The HERE'S HEALTH ALTERNATIVE *Chocolate Book*

HERE'S HEALTH

The ALTERNATIVE Chocolate Book

JANETTE MARSHALL

CENTURY

LONDON   MELBOURNE   AUCKLAND   JOHANNESBURG

Copyright © Here's Health 1986

First published in Great Britain in 1986 by Century Hutchinson Ltd
Brookmount House, 62-65 Chandos Place, Covent Garden,
London WC2N 4NW

Century Hutchinson Publishing Group (Australia) Pty Ltd,
16–22 Church Street, Hawthorn, Melbourne, Victoria 3122

Century Hutchinson Group (NZ) Ltd
32–34 View Road, PO Box 40–086, Glenfield, Auckland 10

Century Hutchinson Group (SA) Pty Ltd
PO Box 337, Bergvlei 2012, South Africa

Designed by Linde Hardaker
Photographs by Ian O'Leary
Home Economist: Judy Bugg
Stylist: Carol Pastor
Carob illustrations by Judith Gauden
Marzipan Slices illustration by Janette Marshall

Marbled paper goods, from The Italian Papershop, II Brompton Arcade, London SW3
Glassware, china and Indian silk, from Liberty, Regent Street
Materials, from Osborne & Little, 304 King's Road, London SW3
Hand-made ceramics, from The Craftsmen Potters, 7 Marshall Street, London W1
Cutlery, from Dickins & Jones, Regent Street, London W1
Tablecloths and napkins, from Descamps, 197 Sloane Street, Knightsbridge, London SW1
Bombe mould, loaned from Covent Garden Kitchen Supplies, 3 North Row, The Market, WC2

Photoset by Rowland Phototypesetting Ltd
Bury St Edmunds, Suffolk
Printed in Italy by New Interlitho

British Library Cataloguing in Publication Data

Marshall, Janette
    The Here's Health alternative chocolate book: over
    100 healthy carob recipes.
    1. Cookery (Carob)
    I. Title
    641.6'446   TX813.C3

ISBN 0 7126 9449 8

Introduction   7
Chocolate   7
Carob and its Advantages   12
Notes on the Recipes   17

The Classics   19
Cakes   35
Biscuits   49
Petits Fours   59
Pâtisserie   63
Desserts & Gâteaux   75
Ice-Cream   97
Making Ice-Cream   98

Children's Corner   103
Drinks   111
Appendices   115
Index   127

Contents

Welcome

to *The Alternative Chocolate Book*. If you are thinking that the only alternative to chocolate is *no* chocolate, then this book and its many recipes will come as a happy surprise to you. For, instead of banning chocolate it introduces carob, the fruit of the Mediterranean carob tree, which has been called 'the healthy alternative' to chocolate.

Chocolate in all its forms has been described as a 'magnificent obsession', and it is undoubtedly one of the joys of life for those with a sweet tooth. But, as we all know today, many of the ingredients of chocolate – the best-known of which is the sugar that rots that sweet tooth – are bad for us. It also contains caffeine and theobromine (both stimulants which may become addictive), phenylethylamine (which can trigger migraines), tyramine (which can also trigger migraines and allergic reactions) and oxalic acid – which prevents the body using the calcium and zinc needed for healthy skin (and thus encourages spotty skins, especially in teenagers).

Carob, however, contains *none* of these elements and thus is by far the better and healthier choice for all those who like to use chocolate in cooking, but don't want to suffer for it. Obviously not everyone is adversely affected by chocolate, but as with many areas of diet, we are looking for alternatives and a wider choice of food. And the carob pod is made into powder and bars, just as chocolate is; it also performs just as well as chocolate in cooking, giving that chocolate look and texture with a hint of a unique flavour of its own. It is an extremely versatile product and I hope that you will find pleasure – and health – in the following pages.

Chocolate

Chocolate is an international passion, each nationality having its own particular taste for bitter chocolate, milk chocolate, white, fresh cream, plain or filled. In Britain we like it sweeter and creamier, and each year we eat more and more: the latest count was more than half a million tons a year with a total cost of more than £1.5 billion. In fact the British eat more chocolate than any other nation in the EEC. An average of 16½ lb (7.5 kg) *each* a year is eaten in Britain compared with the average for the rest of the EEC of 10½ lb (4.76 kg). These figures from Mintel Market Intelligence also reflect that more than 56 per cent of adults buy some sort of chocolate at least once a week. The consumption has been steadily growing, and has increased by one-fifth since 1981, during which time the amount of money spent on chocolate has also increased by one-third.

A newly published national survey on the eating habits of 15 to 21-year-olds commissioned by the Ministry of Agriculture, Fisheries and Food, showed men in this group to be eating an average of 30 g chocolate a day and women an average of

20 g, with the 15 to 18-year-olds of both sexes being the biggest consumers: 35 g for males and 30 g for females.

It really is a passion and it's obviously an addiction for many 'chocoholics'. How many times have you heard someone say that once they start on a bar or a box they cannot stop until it has all gone? They are not alone, nor unusual, for the passion has been raging for centuries.

The history of chocolate

It probably all started with the Aztecs around AD 600 in the Mexican Yucatan jungles where the first cacao plantations were made. From these trees the cocoa beans were harvested, roasted, ground and combined with liquid to make a frothy drink called *cacahuatl*. When *cacahuatl* was used as a drink during religious ceremonies the liquid used was wine. The Aztecs and their Emperor Montezuma (still a popular name for chocolate products) have been associated with stories of decadence and extravagance, and Montezuma is said to have drunk vanilla-flavoured *cacahuatl* from gold goblets with the favourites of his court – and the court was reputed to have used fifty large jars of the drink each day!

It was not until the Spanish began to plunder the wealth of the ancient South Americans that the taste of chocolate was brought to Europe. The bitter brew was not to the *conquistadores'* taste and at first the Spanish added spices and chillies; they may later have been the first to add sugar to cocoa. The cacao tree began to be planted in Spanish territories, but they kept the secret to themselves because it was not until about a century later, around 1615, that chocolate found its way to the French court. There, along with coffee, it became a fashionable drink, and was viewed by the French wine growers as a threat to the national drink.

By the late 1650s it had become a popular drink over the Channel in Britain, and in London especially the popularity grew with the opening of the first chocolate house in 1657. Coffee houses too proliferated a little later and by the 1700s there were 2,500 in central London, attracting writers, politicians, poets, lawyers, actors, army or navy men, who sat gossiping or gambling, smoking or reading, over their chocolate and coffee. Samuel Pepys wrote in his diary, 'Went to Mr Bland's and there drank my morning draft of good chocollatte.'

As the tax on chocolate was lifted, it became more accessible. Mechanical methods of processing were introduced by John Fry and some eighty years later, in 1884, with the introduction of John Cadbury's special recipe drinking chocolate, it became a national breakfast and bedtime beverage. Today it is still a grand passion, with world 'grindings' (that rather odd stock-market term for cocoa consumption) at 1.7 million tonnes in 1985.

Cocoa, tea and coffee are so much a feature of everyday life that it is difficult to imagine what people drank before. Often it was ale, wine or other alcoholic drinks, so tea, coffee and drinking chocolate were providing useful alternatives. Today, however, when we have far more choice in food and drink, we have also become aware of some of the problems that can be associated with these stimulating beverages.

Chocolate and caffeine

In the case of chocolate, for example, it contains caffeine and theobromine which are, chemically speaking, methyl derivatives of xanthine, or, to you and me, stimulants. Caffeine is the most active of the two and it works directly on the brain, prompting enhanced sensory perception, inspiration and alertness. That is why it is used in drugs and over-the-counter medicines which are anti-soporific or 'pick-you-ups'. This can obviously be useful, but caffeine may also be addictive, and over-use can often encourage the cup of coffee – cigarette – alcohol syndrome which is not so easy to break.

Although caffeine also has analgesic (pain-killing) properties, it is not widely used in that sense because of its side-effects: anxiety, nervousness, tension, nausea – even palpitations. For, in stimulating the brain and activating other organs, caffeine also has a direct effect on the heart: it increases its rate, which is why some heavy coffee drinkers experience palpitations. Because no two people are the same, everyone has their own caffeine tolerance or intolerance level, and smaller amounts that would not affect some may cause palpitations in others. Caffeine can also make the heart more sensitive to emotional factors, thus causing irregular heart rhythms, or it can provoke emotional-type reactions leaving the person shaky, weak and 'emotional'.

Caffeine also stimulates the gastric juices, which is why coffee is a popular after-dinner drink, but taken throughout the day – as it is in chocolate, confectionery, tea, coffee, soft drinks and cola drinks – it exposes the body to constant stimulation. Its strong diuretic properties cause the body to excrete more fluid than might be necessary, thus leaching the body of valuable water-soluble vitamin C and the B vitamins.

Some recent research has shown that caffeine can also cause a significant rise in blood-fat levels, especially cholesterol. This is one type of fat that we do not want circulating in the blood because it increases the risk of deposition as arterial plaque – a factor in heart disease. Norwegian research has suggested that by giving up caffeine, cholesterol levels can be lowered more effectively than through a low-fat diet. More recent research from Israel suggests that men in particular could be at greater risk of heart attacks if caffeine is proved to be the factor that raised blood-cholesterol levels. A study using 1,007 men and 589 women from Jerusalem reported a definite link between coffee drinking and raised cholesterol levels. Men who drank five or more cups a day had the highest of raised cholesterol levels, but blood fats were less affected by coffee intake in women. Tea had no significant effect on levels of blood fats, even though it contains caffeine.

Caffeine has also been shown to stimulate the release of the body's stored energy reserves which results in sugars being released into the blood. In conjunction with high blood fat this brings increased risk, not only of heart disease but also of other 'modern diseases of civilisation', such as diabetes. Releasing sugars that may not be burned up by the body's energy requirements (the amount of calories needed) could also lead to weight gain and ultimately obesity. To explain further: the body's energy stores of fat are usually only released by stimulants such as fasting or increased physical activity like aerobic exercise, when the calories are burned up. But if you stimulate the release of sugars by taking tea, coffee or chocolate and continue to sit in front of the tv or at your desk, then you are not burning up the released calories and they are likely to be deposited as fat. As one in three of us is overweight, according to government statistics, it is not too fanciful to hypothesize some link between obesity and our passion for caffeine.

Expectant mothers have also been advised to watch the amount of caffeine in their diets. American doctors suggest that pregnant women limit their intake to just two cups of coffee a day. In this country the Ministry of Agriculture, Fisheries and Food's Advisory Committee sought advice on the safety of caffeine as a food ingredient or additive from the DHSS. As a result expectant mothers were advised, through the Health Education Council, to limit caffeine intake during pregnancy to prevent premature births or babies with poorer reflexes than normal.

By raising the blood-sugar levels, caffeine may also contribute to the vicious circle of swings in mood associated with refined, sugary foods which often results in low blood sugar. Confectionery snacks and sugary foods and drinks make great demands on the pancreas to increase insulin production: this is needed to clear the bloodstream of the sudden influx of sugars. Because the sugars enter the bloodstream quickly the confectionery producers argue that they give the body instant energy. This is far from the case, however. Such a sudden release of energy results in a panic situation and demands an instant, large dose of insulin from the pancreas; this clears the sugars very quickly and efficiently, but results in hypoglycaemia (low blood sugar) after a sugary snack or meal. You may know the symptoms – an urge for something sweet (very often a chocolate craving) followed by a hollow feeling soon after eating, accompanied by dizziness, sometimes irritability, and the desire for yet another sweet snack. This vicious circle is also typically associated with a diet high in fat and sugar and low in fibre: unrefined carbohydrate (high fibre) foods produce a steadier stream of energy and sugars to the bloodstream, making you feel satisfied for longer, without any hypoglycaemic effects.

Caffeine has also been linked to benign breast disease (lumpy, painful and swollen breasts, usually as part of pre-menstrual syndrome prior to menstruation). This is because the methylxanthines caffeine and theobromine encourage the binding of the hormone prolactin to the breast which is responsible for the cystic lumps typical of this problem.

Chocolate and spots

The suggestion that scientists have found no links between teenage acne, spots and chocolate is one with which many people would argue. Teenagers, like younger children, have higher than average requirements for calcium because they are growing rapidly, and calcium is needed to build healthy teeth and bones and maintain nerves and muscles. (Incidentally the elderly and nursing mums also need extra calcium.) Calcium is also needed to help control the level of fats in our blood. Chocolate proponents say that because chocolate is high in calcium (carob is higher), it is therefore good for the skin and general health, but this fails to take into account the large amounts of oxalic acid present in chocolate. This inhibits the absorption of calcium, which in turn is needed for the use of zinc – a trace element vital for healthy skin. Too much oxalic acid could lead to a calcium deficiency which may cause rickets in the very young and osteoporosis and osteomalacia in the elderly. These latter diseases result in the easily fractured and broken bones of the elderly and the curvatures of the spine that result in hunched backs, as well as muscle weakness and spasms. Oxalic acid is found in high concentrations in rhubarb and spinach, and has also been incriminated in the formation of certain types of kidney stones because oxalates can combine with calcium oxalates, the basis of some kidney stones.

Zinc is needed for many functions in the body apart from healthy skin. It is especially needed for cell growth, and lack of zinc can lead to slow growth in children. It is also vital for healthy reproduction. Diets high in refined white flour and sugar products often lack zinc which is found in unprocessed foods like whole grains and wholemeal bread, seafood and some meat and eggs.

As school tuck-shops often stock chocolate bars and other confectionery rather than fresh fruit or savoury snacks, teenage skin problems are likely to be aggravated. In the survey of 15 to 21 year olds' eating habits, chocolate was mentioned by 18 per cent of people who named favourite foods they felt they should not eat (among dieters the figure was 23 per cent). When asked why they should not eat chocolate the main reason given was because it caused spots and bad skin.

Chocolate and tooth decay

There have been claims by the National Institute for Dental Research in America that chocolate can *prevent* tooth decay. It is said that chocolate's fat content (about six times higher than carob's) inhibits the decay-causing effects of the sugar in chocolate, by coating the teeth with a protective layer of fat which prevents the acid-producing bacteria, which feed on sugar in the mouth, from attacking the enamel of the teeth. Considering chocolate is 60 per cent sugar (and Mars bars and similar confectionery 65 per cent), and sugar is the main cause of tooth decay, eating chocolate is hardly likely to prevent tooth decay. And the more 'confectionery occasions' (to coin a confectionery trade phrase) you have in your day, the more sugary fuel for the enamel-attacking bacteria (for frequency is almost worse than quantity).

Phenylethylamine, tyramine and chocolate

If the spots and tooth decay don't get you, there are other ingredients in chocolate that might: phenylethylamine and tyramine, both of which have been found to trigger migraines or headaches in some people, and may be responsible for putting chocolate near the top of the table of the most common food allergens, along with wheat, milk and eggs. Phenylethylamine may also be the culprit behind the myth that chocolate is an aphrodisiac.

These powers were probably first bestowed upon chocolate by Montezuma who allegedly drank *cacahuatl* before visiting his harem, and used the same drink at religious ceremonies dedicated to Xochiquetzal, goddess of love. Many centuries later Madame du Barry offered chocolate to her male consorts, and Casanova thought he seduced women with the help of chocolate (he did not have the *Milk Tray* man's approach: he ate the chocolate himself before visiting the ladies in question!). Today this association is continued in advertisements that encourage gifts of chocolates to lovers, but the aphrodisiac power has never been, as far as I know, put on trial – double blind or even cupid blind! It could be that the phenylethylamine is of more use to the *thwarted* lover than the active lover, because the substance also occurs naturally in the brain. Fluctuations of emotion characteristic of those in love are directly related to the amount of phenylethylamine in the body. When we are suffering the kind of depression associated with falling out of love or experiencing thwarted love, levels of phenylethylamine are low in the brain, so eating chocolate may deliver extra doses and give some temporary solace – until the spots step in . . .

The reaction which triggers migraines is caused by tyramine (an amine of the amino acid tyrosine) stimulating the sympathetic nervous system, causing high rises in blood pressure. Tyramine is also present in cheese and some red wine and it is usually destroyed by substances in the body called monoamine oxidases. There is more tyramine in Cheddar cheese than there is in chocolate and so this problem is often medically referred to as the 'cheese reaction'. Some anti-depressant drugs inhibit monoamine oxidases' activity which is why cheese and chocolate are not allowed to be taken in conjunction with certain drugs.

Carob and its Advantages

Carob contains no caffeine, no theobromine, no phenylethylamine, no tyramine and no oxalic acid. Carob is naturally sweeter than cocoa powder and therefore does not need the addition of large amounts of refined sugar – in fact it is available in no-added-sugar versions. Carob powder is also free from the additives and salt found in some cocoa powders and invariably in most drinking chocolates, which also contain added sugar. The fibre content of carob is also greater than cocoa, and carob contains the digestion-regulating fibres pectin and lignin (although neither is really significant in nutritional terms because carob's contribution to the diet is very small – unless, of course, you feast on carob pods).

Carob contains vitamins A and D and three of the important B vitamins. It is also high in calcium, phosphorus and potassium. Phosphorus, like calcium, is needed for healthy teeth and bones. It is also involved in complicated chemical reactions that allow us to burn up calories as energy, and it is also needed so that we can use vitamin B_{12}—especially important for vegetarians. Potassium is linked with sodium (salt) in the diet and there should be more potassium than sodium in our food; generally speaking we eat too much salt, and cocoa contains 700 milligrams sodium per 100 grams compared with 100 mg per 100 g in carob powder.

What is carob?

The carob tree is a member of the legume (or pea) family. The genus species is *ceratonia siliqua* which belongs to the sub-family *caesalpinoideae* of the *leguminosae*. It grows all over the Mediterranean and also in the United States, imported by the US Patent Office in 1854 from Alicante, Spain and in 1859 from Palestine. In Spain (the largest producer) 200,000 tons of fruit were produced in 1982. Spain is followed by Italy and then Cyprus in the commercial production league. In Greece there were 3½ million trees, 83 per cent of them in Crete at the time of the Mitrakos Report in 1968, when 35,000 tons were produced.

The carob tree prefers a dry Mediterranean climate and a calcium-rich soil. It can withstand some salinity and does not grow at altitudes above 500 metres (whereas the cacao tree grows best in the intense heat and moisture of a tropical climate). The arid conditions favoured by the carob tree are also naturally alien to fungus and pests, so the trees need little or no chemical sprays and are naturally free from disease and pests.

There are 200 varieties of carob tree but the *ceratonia siliqua* is the variety best for edible carob because it has good flavour and texture (some carob fruit is completely flavourless). It can take 20 years for the tree to reach its full height of 40–50 feet (12–15 metres) and 15 years for fruit to be produced regularly. However, it will go on producing beans for more than 60 years and a really large tree can produce a ton of beans from one harvest.

Flowering takes place during September and October, and sometimes a 'winter' flowering occurs. The flowers, seen alongside the fruits of the previous season, grow in clusters on the branches of the female trees in the midst of foliage, and must be pollinated by pollen from flowers on male trees. The blossom of the latter is attractive with long reddish threads hanging down from the flower, and for this reason male trees are often used in landscape gardens (and they have no pods to litter the ground).

At first the developing carob pods look like green broad beans but as they mature the leathery pods turn a dark chocolate brown with a glossy surface. They can be 4–10 inches (10–25 cm) long, and weigh ¾–1½ oz (18–40 g). Once ripe they fall from the trees and are harvested between September and November. The mealy pods contain four series of oval holes, each bearing a seed similar in appearance to a watermelon seed. Each pod can contain up to fifteen seeds.

The carob harvest

After harvesting the pods are processed, usually in the country of origin. Firstly they are both dry- and wet-cleaned and then broken coarsely (kibbled) to separate the seeds from the pulp. The seeds or kernels are then processed to make a natural gum called locust bean gum (ceratonia gum or carob bean gum) which is used in ice-creams, dessert fruit fillings, cartoned salads, salad dressings, desserts and other products as a gelling agent, stabilizer or emulsifier. You might see it on product labels under its name, or as additive number E410. It may also be used as a thickener in pharmaceuticals and cosmetics.

Interestingly, Ancient Egyptians also made use of the gummy properties of the carob seed by using it as an adhesive in binding mummies, and the pods and seeds have been found in Egyptian tombs. Today the gum may also be mixed with tragacanth gums (E413) which exude from the trunk and branches of another species of the pea family, *astragalus gummifer*, and this is also used as a stabilizer, emulsifier, thickener or to prevent sugar crystallization in confectionery. An oil called algaroba is also extracted from the carob seeds or kernels to be used for medical purposes, and an ancient Egyptian temple at Idfu is said to have contained medical prescriptions which used essential oil of carob.

After the seeds have been extracted, the pod is roasted and this is a carefully controlled operation. It has to be at a temperature high enough to inactivate the enzyme lipase: this would otherwise ferment with the vegetable oils in the product and cause saponification (the conversion of a fat into a soap by the addition of an alkali) which would give carob a soapy taste. Roasting also eliminates bacteria and reduces the moisture content allowing the roasted kibbles to be milled and sieved. The roasting will also determine the colour and flavour of the carob, and while the temperature has to be high enough to inactivate lipase it must not be so high that it produces a dark and unappealing colour.

After roasting, milling and sieving, the carob powder (or flour as it is sometimes called) is tested for bacteriological purity. Because it is hydrophilic – attracts water – it is stored in controlled conditions to prevent it becoming hard and lumpy.

The carob powder is then ready for use in baking and food manufacture, or it is made into bars by mixing with raw cane sugar, vegetable fats, skimmed milk powder, lecithin (a natural emulsifier) and flavouring. In some carob bars other flavourings such as mint or orange oils are used, and fruit and nuts can be added just as they are in the production of chocolate confectionery. The addition of sugar is unnecessary because carob is naturally sweet, and no-added-sugar products are available. There are also non-dairy carob bars which use vegetable fat, soya flour and soya lecithin as an emulsifier. Carob which is not processed for human consumption is used as animal feed.

The history of carob

Those who were children during the Second World War may have come across carob pods as an alternative to sweets and chocolate. There are no official records of how much was eaten or what was available, because carob was not a controlled food, so we have only memories. There is evidence, however, that it was used by the people of southern Greece during the German occupation as a food source, and Wellington's cavalry are said to have been sustained by it in the Peninsular campaign. The British cavalry are also thought to have made the same use of carob when stationed in Malta in the 1800s.

The sustaining power of carob may – or may not – be seen in the Bible. John the Baptist lived on locusts and wild honey in the wilderness, and many scholars believe the locusts to have been carob pods, not insects, because locust bean is another name for carob. (Yet another is St John's Bread – because of this story – which becomes Johannesbrot in parts of Europe.) Some theologians disagree with this, though, citing the habits of desert nomads who do not hesitate to eat locusts and grasshoppers. This latter argument is linked with the apocryphal *Gospel of the Ebionites* which substitutes for the word *akris* (locust) the word *egkris*, which is a cake made with oil and honey (probably some kind of *halva*). It has been suggested that the Ebionites' vegetarianism made them remove the reference to locusts which may thus have lead to the locust bean/carob connection.

Yet carob is also thought to have made another Biblical appearance as the husks referred to in *Luke* 15:16, the parable of the prodigal son. The younger son who wastes his portion becomes a servant and is sent to feed the swine: 'And he would fain have filled his belly with the husks that the swine did eat; and no man gave unto him.' In times of famine and drought carob trees are known to still produce crops and their husks (or pods) would probably have been the only available animal feed.

The carob tree is also referred to in the *Talmud*. There is a story of a young rabbi who came upon an old man planting a carob seed beside the road. When the rabbi remarked that the old man would be dead long before the tree bore fruit the old man replied that he planted for those who came after him. The young rabbi then lay down to rest and did not awake for seventy years by which time the tree was full of fruit and he was an old man in unfamiliar surroundings.

The Greek Theophrastus in 4 BC recorded that his contemporaries called the carob the Egyptian fig, and the Romans are said to have eaten the pods when green and fresh for their natural sweetness. According to Pliny, if dried they needed a couple of days soaking before eating.

Our word for carob is derived from the Old French *carouge* which in turn comes from the mediaeval Latin *carrubia*, taken from the Arabic *karruba*. The etymology of the word is also linked with the Arabic *kirat* which was the weight of four grains derived from the old Greek κεράτιον meaning fruit of the carob. The four grains would have been four of the seeds or kernels which became the standard measure for gold because they were renowned for their uniformity of weight. Thus from the Arabic *kirat*, we have the modern word *carat* which is still the international standard for gold – all from the humble and healthy carob! The inedible seeds themselves may have been used as coins at one time in the Levant, and the Egyptian word for sweetness is also said to have etymological connections with their word for carob.

Cooking with carob

Carob as we know it in Britain today has no such exotic connections. It was primarily used as an alternative to chocolate by the health movement in the late 60s and 70s in California. A carob product called *Kalibu* was brought from California and bought by the Holgran group of health-food companies in 1981 when its retail turnover was £⅓ million. Today the retail turnover is £3 million.

The product has been improved since its original introduction and has just been reformulated to make it darker and richer. Those who already eat a 'wholefood' diet using less sugar and fat, have preferred the no-added-sugar varieties in blind tastings, say the manufacturers, but for those with a sweeter tooth, accustomed to conventional confectionery, the variety with added raw cane sugar is usually preferred. Carob can obviously be eaten as a 'treat' – as chocolate is – but *occasionally* must be the emphasis. With carob, just as with chocolate, if it replaces nutritious foods, especially at lunchtime (or even breakfast with many children), then the diet becomes disrupted. A balanced and sensible diet should *not* have a place for regular, daily 'confectionery occasions' as the manufacturers and advertisers of chocolate confectionery encourage.

For cooking, both plain and no-added-sugar carob bars can be bought as well as carob powder. They are used in the same way as chocolate and cocoa, and can replace them in many recipes. There are plans to produce larger blocks of carob for cooking and catering purposes and carob chips are available in some health-food shops (where carob is usually bought). Like chocolate chips they are teardrop shaped, and most health-food shop proprietors pack their own as they are not yet sold under any brand name. They are not as shiny as chocolate chips because they 'scuff' easily, giving them the appearance of chocolate bloom (the whitish appearance on chocolate when the fat has risen to the surface).

Because carob is naturally sweet it may allow you to reduce the amount of sugar in your recipes, and using carob is as simple as using cocoa powder or chocolate. In some uses it is *simpler* than chocolate. For example, when covering or dipping items in carob it does not have to be tempered (heated to no more than 120°F/49°C, cooled while stirring to 80°F/27°C then re-heated to 90°F/32°C) like chocolate couverture (covering chocolate). You can simply break it up and melt it in a basin in a pan of hot water or in a double boiler; adding a small amount of vegetable oil or white vegetable fat will break it down, making it easier for dipping and spreading. The only disadvantage of carob is that it does not have the glossy, shiny appearance of chocolate; it lacks the fat of cocoa butter that gives chocolate this characteristic. However, a tablespoon of skimmed milk powder diluted in hot water and added to the melted carob will achieve an excellent sheen.

You can even melt carob bars in a microwave oven by breaking them up, placing them in a suitable dish (not a metal dish or one with a metallic glaze), and using the oven on a high setting for about 1 minute. (Check your own oven for best results because microwave ovens vary when it comes to power settings, unlike standardized gas or electric settings.)

Carob powder should be sieved before use, even if it does not appear to be lumpy, because, like sieving flour, it helps to introduce more air to baking, even more vital when using wholemeal ingredients. But beware, carob powder tends to be more 'fly-away' than cocoa powder, so do not shoot it directly into the electric mixing bowl while the machine is in operation or you will end up with a carob dust-storm in the kitchen! Fold it in gently to start off with.

Carob and the future

Finally, it is interesting to think of possible carob uses beyond the culinary. Carob might also have a lot to offer world ecology. At a time when deforestation is threatening world climate and agriculture, carob could become a major crop. Leading organic expert, Lawrence D. Hills, singles out the carob tree as particularly suitable for mass cultivation on dry hillside Mediterranean areas. There it would need, or rob the soil of, little moisture, and it would prevent soil erosion and provide valuable forest coverage. It would also give a high crop yield, according to Hills: 'No other crop will produce so much food to the acre from the same kind of land with such low rainfall.' He bases his comments on an analysis of carob pods' nutritional values in *Rations for Livestock* (HMSO), which shows carob to be 70 per cent carbohydrate, 4 per cent protein and 9 per cent fibre.

Australian agriculturists agree with this view, and carob could be invaluable in replacing shrubs and trees in the 'dead heart' of Australia. This has been burnt out by bush fires, some accidental, some started by Aborigines to clear the eucalyptus forests to improve the growth of kangaroo grass and thus encourage an increase in the number of kangaroos for game. Carob trees could provide the same shade for kangaroos as kangaroo grass and, while withstanding the drought and measure of salt in the soil, they could also provide a valuable crop for use as mineral-rich animal fodder, organic fertilizer and to produce carob powder and bars. I'm sure Kanga, Roo and Pooh would approve!

Notes on the Recipes

Beside each of the carob recipes for chocolate classics is a comparison of the nutritional content of the original chocolate versions and the new carob version. For a detailed comparison of the nutritional content, see pages 116–126. This is designed to show not only the absence of some of the less desirable ingredients of chocolate, such as caffeine and theobromine, but also that by making a few other simple changes to the way you bake and the ingredients you use you can make your dishes 'healthier': you can raise the amount of fibre in them and cut the amount of fat, sugar and salt used, which also results in lower calorie foods.

The changes are quite simple and ones that I have for many years successfully used in my cookery books and home food preparation. A simple summary is given below.

★ 100% wholemeal flour is used in all the recipes except those for choux pastry where 81% is used. When sieving flour, always add the bran from the sieve to the mixture.

★ The amount of fat is reduced as far as possible, and where fat is used soft vegetable margarines – which are high in polyunsaturates – are generally the first choice. If this rule is applied to everyday eating then the few recipes which specifically require butter should not upset a 'balanced diet'. Where butter is used it is unsalted.

★ The amount of sugar is reduced, especially when compared with conventional recipes, and often honey or fructose (fruit sugar) are used. Both have a greater sweetening power and thus require less to be added than when making the same dish with white sugar. Fructose is also considered less disruptive to blood sugar levels than refined sugars. In some recipes raw cane sugars are used: it is argued by some that they are better because they contain minerals and vitamins not found in white sugar, but their contribution is nutritionally insignificant, I think. I use them because they are superior products – especially good brands such as Billingtons.

★ Jams in the recipes are no-added-sugar jams pioneered by Whole Earth which have the flavour of fruit purées and are very versatile.

★ Strained Greek yoghurt is used in place of double or whipping cream, sometimes on its own, and sometimes in recipes which use gelatine (or agar agar if preferred) to make piping creams that have a fraction of the calories and fat of cream. The recipes in *The Alternative Chocolate Book* use powdered gelatine, ½ oz/12 g of which is equal to 3 teaspoonfuls; using agar agar instead, you will need only 1–2 teaspoonfuls to set the same amount of liquid. I prefer a softer set using 1 teaspoonful, but to be on the firmer (or safer) side, you might like to use 2 teaspoonfuls. Gelozone, the other vegetable setting agent, will also require 2 teaspoonfuls.

★ Low-fat cheeses such as skimmed milk cheese, quark and low-fat curd cheese replace the cream cheeses often used in cheesecake recipes. They are also used along with yoghurt in ice cream, soufflé or mousse recipes to give a creamy texture without the fat and calories.

★ Decaffeinated coffee is used where a coffee or mocha flavour is required for the recipe.

★ Skimmed milk is used in place of full-cream milk.

★ Natural essences are used for flavouring dishes rather than laboratory-created artificial flavourings.

★ Free-range eggs are used in all my recipes because I think they are a better product.

★ A salt-free baking powder will cut down further on sodium in the diet.

★ Plain carob bars come in two varieties: no added sugar and a regular plain made with raw cane sugar.

★ And don't forget to sieve the carob powder before use.

REMEMBER if you have not baked with wholemeal flour before, or are not used to recipes with less fat and sugar, the cakes and bakes will not be as light and fluffy as white products.

Although my roots were in the conventional Cordon Bleu approach to cooking, I now much prefer the textures, flavours and general results of this healthier approach to food and cooking.

STOP PRESS Strained yoghurt from Cyprus is also now available in both regular and low-fat varieties which offers even more opportunity to cut down on fat.

Sophisticated chocolate favourites such as Black Forest Gâteau, dark and delicious Sachertorte, mousses and profiteroles can all be hugely successful using carob instead of chocolate.

They are also nutritionally better when made with wholemeal flour, less sugar, and less saturated fats – which arc replaced with soft vegetable margarines, high in poly-unsaturatcs. In addition, yoghurt-based creams and fillings replace high-calorie and high-fat double cream.

The nutritional analysis summarized in the tables shown alongside the ten classic recipes highlights the nutritional value of the carob version as against the traditional chocolate versions. The carob versions have a higher fibre content and a generally lower fat, sugar and salt content, together with a good mineral content and an absence of caffeine and theobromine.

The Classics

Black Forest Gâteau

SERVES 8

Britain's favourite dessert and ubiquitous on sweet trolleys, but it is usually mass-produced and flavourless. This version is lower in fat and sugar, but a lot higher on flavour. Top with fresh cherries for a special occasion.

4 free-range eggs
4 oz/100 g clear honey
5 oz/150 g wholemeal flour
1 teaspoon salt-free baking powder
1 oz/25 g carob powder
1 × 60 g bar no-added-sugar plain carob, broken into pieces
2 tablespoons strong black decaffeinated coffee

filling and decoration
8 oz/225 g strained Greek yoghurt
no-added-sugar black cherry jam
1 quantity Chantilly Piping Cream (p. 23–3)
1 × 60 g bar plain carob
fresh cherries

Lightly oil an 8-in (20-cm) cake tin and set the oven to 350°F/180°C/Gas 4. Whisk the eggs and honey together until thick and ropy in consistency. Sieve the flour, baking powder and carob powder together. Melt the carob with the coffee gently in the top of a double boiler or in a basin standing in a

NUTRITIONAL COMPARISON TABLE		
	Carob Black Forest Gâteau	*Chocolate Black Forest Gâteau*
CALORIES	2501	4185
CARBOHYDRATE	283	523
FAT	107	226
PROTEIN	108	68
FIBRE	16	4
SODIUM	1340	1277
POTASSIUM	2566	2160
IRON	35	11
CAFFEINE	—	0·175
THEOBROMINE	—	1·055

The Classics

pan of hot water, then whisk into the egg mixture. Carefully fold in the flour and pour into the prepared tin. Bake for 35 minutes until an inserted skewer comes out clean. Cool completely before decorating the cake.

Cut the cake horizontally into 2 or 3 slices and sandwich together with strained yoghurt and black cherry jam. Mask the top and sides of the cake with Chantilly Piping Cream, leaving a little for piping, then press some grated carob onto the sides. Pipe noisettes or curls of cream around the edge of the cake. Pile some carob caraque (see p. 96 for how to make) in the centre, and top alternate noisettes with a fresh cherry.

The Classics

Carob Profiteroles

MAKES 16

¼ pint/150 ml water
2 oz/50 g unsalted butter
3 oz/75 g 81% wholemeal flour
2 free-range eggs, lightly beaten

Chantilly piping cream

½ oz/12 g gelatine
4 tablespoons boiling water
8 oz/225 g strained Greek yoghurt
2 drops natural vanilla essence
1 free-range egg white

hot carob sauce

1 × 60 g bar no-added-sugar plain carob, broken into pieces
4 tablespoons skimmed milk
1 tablespoon skimmed milk powder

Lightly oil a baking sheet and set the oven to 400°F/200°C/Gas 6. Fit a piping bag with a ½-in (12-mm) plain nozzle.

For the choux pastry, place the water and butter in a saucepan and bring to the boil. Remove from the heat and stir until the butter has melted. Sieve the flour twice, then beat vigorously with a wooden spoon into the butter and water until the mixture forms a thick paste and leaves the sides of the pan in a shiny ball. Leave to cool for 3 minutes then gradually beat in the egg, a little at a time, beating well between additions. Do not let the paste

NUTRITIONAL COMPARISON TABLE		
	Carob Profiteroles	*Chocolate Profiteroles*
CALORIES	1570	3097
CARBOHYDRATE	131	348
FAT	95	178
PROTEIN	76	35
FIBRE	6	3
SODIUM	1164	1471
POTASSIUM	1837	804
IRON	10	9
CAFFEINE	—	0·06
THEOBROMINE	—	0·35

The Classics

become too soft because it must hold its shape when piped: omit a little of the egg, if necessary. Place the paste in the piping bag and pipe mounds onto the prepared baking sheet. Bake for 15 minutes then reduce heat to 350°F/180°C/Gas 4 for a further 10 minutes.

Remove from the oven and allow to cool on a wire tray. If no splits have occurred naturally at the base or sides of the buns, pierce them to allow the steam to escape and to give an incision into which the cream filling may be piped when the pastry is cold.

To make the Chantilly piping cream sprinkle the gelatine onto the water and stir until it is dissolved. Leave to cool and, when on the point of setting, stir into the yoghurt with the vanilla essence. Whisk the egg white until it forms stiff peaks and fold into the mixture. Chill before piping into the profiteroles.

To make the hot carob sauce, melt the carob in the top of a double boiler or in a basin standing in a pan of hot water. Mix the milk and milk powder together and warm to dissolve the milk powder. Stir into the melting carob and continue to stir for a few minutes until shiny. Pour over the filled profiteroles at once, and serve immediately.

The Classics

Boston Brownies

MAKES 9

4 oz/100 g soft margarine
4 oz/100 g light muscovado sugar
2 free-range eggs, lightly beaten
2 oz/50 g wholemeal flour
1 oz/25 g carob powder
1 teaspoon salt-free baking powder
3 oz/75 g chopped walnuts
9 walnut halves
a little no-added-sugar jam

Lightly oil an 8-in (20-cm) square cake tin, and set the oven to 350°F/180°C/ Gas 4.

Cream together the margarine and sugar until light and fluffy. Gradually beat in the eggs. Sieve the flour, carob powder and baking powder together and fold into the mixture with the chopped nuts. Spoon into the prepared tin and bake for 30–35 minutes until an inserted skewer comes out clean. Remove from the oven and leave to cool.

Cut into squares and place half a walnut on top of each square, fixing in place with a smear of jam.

NUTRITIONAL COMPARISON TABLE

	Boston Brownies	Chocolate Brownies
CALORIES	2092	2370
CARBOHYDRATE	157	170
FAT	191	214
PROTEIN	34	42
FIBRE	12	8
SODIUM	1453	1893
POTASSIUM	1444	1803
IRON	23	12
CAFFEINE	—	0·13
THEOBROMINE	—	0·74

The Classics

Box clever with the classic Boston Brownies, page 24

Three gorgeous gâteaus. *From the back:* Dark and delicious Carob
Mousse Gâteau, a rich mousse between orange tortes, pages 90–1;
Carob Slice, page 78; and Hazelnut Gâteau with nutty sides and
smooth frosting, page 77

Ordinary profiteroles can't hold a torch to low-calorie Carob Profiteroles, pages 22–3, with Hot Carob Sauce

Relax to a Strauss record and enjoy a decaffeinated coffee and a slice of Carob Sachertorte, page 25

Carob Sachertorte

SERVES 6

4 oz/100 g soft margarine
3 oz/75 g fructose
1½ × 60 g bars no-added-sugar plain carob, broken into pieces
3 free-range eggs, separated
4 oz/100 g wholemeal flour, sieved
carob ganache
2 × 60 g bars no-added-sugar plain carob, broken into pieces
¼ pint/150 ml single cream

Lightly oil a 7-in (17.5-cm) cake tin and line with greaseproof paper. Set the oven to 325°F/160°C/Gas 3.

Cream together the margarine and fructose until pale and fluffy. Melt the carob by placing in the top of a double boiler or in a basin standing in a pan of hot water. Remove from the heat and cool a little before mixing with the margarine and fructose. Beat in the egg yolks and the flour. Whisk the egg whites until stiff and holding firm peaks. Fold in 2 tablespoons of white to lighten the mixture, then fold in the remaining whites. Pour into the prepared tin and bake for 45 minutes. When cooked remove from the oven and allow to cool on a wire cooling tray. To make the carob ganache, melt the carob using the method above. Stir in the single cream and mix well, then whisk or beat until the mixture thickens and becomes shiny – do not heat above 110°F/43°C. It can then be spooned over the cake. It will be thick enough to set, but of a consistency that will run from the top of the cake, down the sides to give a smooth covering. Reserve a little and pipe the word 'Sacher', or 'Sachertorte', on top of the cake.

NUTRITIONAL COMPARISON TABLE		
	Carob Sachertorte	*Chocolate Sachertorte*
CALORIES	2934	3992
CARBOHYDRATE	247	428
FAT	263	232
PROTEIN	57	68
FIBRE	11	3
SODIUM	1541	1421
POTASSIUM	1934	1663
IRON	25	11
CAFFEINE	—	0·195
THEOBROMINE	—	1·137

The Classics

Carob Fudge Cake

SERVES 8–10

1 oz/25 g carob powder
¼ pint/150 ml water
1½ × 60 g bars no-added-sugar plain carob, broken into pieces
4 oz/100 g soft margarine
4 oz/100 g light muscovado sugar
3 free-range eggs
1 tablespoon decaffeinated instant coffee dissolved in 1 tablespoon water
8 oz/225 g wholemeal flour, sieved

fudge frosting
2 × 60 g bars plain carob, broken into pieces
8 oz/225 g low-fat curd cheese

Lightly oil and line with greaseproof paper an 8-in (20-cm) cake tin, and set the oven to 350°F/180°C/Gas 4.

Mix together the carob powder and the water. Melt the carob pieces by placing in the top of a double boiler or in a basin standing in a pan of hot water. Remove from the heat. Cream together the margarine and sugar until light and fluffy. Lightly beat the eggs and add gradually to the margarine, adding a little flour if the mixture curdles. Add the coffee and water with the melted carob to the margarine mixture. Fold in the flour and pour the mixture into the prepared tin, levelling the top. Bake for 40 minutes or until an inserted skewer comes out clean.

The Classics

Cool on a wire cooling tray and when completely cold cut in half horizontally. To make the frosting, melt 1½ of the carob bars in the top of a double boiler or in a basin standing in a pan of hot water. Beat the curd cheese to soften it. Pour the melted carob into the cheese and, working quickly, cream them together. With a palette knife, fill and cover the top and sides of the cake before the frosting stiffens too much. Pattern the top using the palette knife, and sprinkle if liked with the remaining half bar of carob, grated.

NUTRITIONAL COMPARISON TABLE

	Carob Fudge Cake	Chocolate Fudge Cake
CALORIES	3391	5677
CARBOHYDRATE	350	605
FAT	185	1015
PROTEIN	100	74
FIBRE	22	—
SODIUM	2281	2639
POTASSIUM	2322	2896
IRON	42	24
CAFFEINE	—	0·086
THEOBROMINE	—	0·28

The Classics

Carob Digestives

MAKES 10

4 oz/100 g wholemeal flour
½ teaspoon salt-free baking powder
1 oz/25 g light muscovado sugar
2 oz/50 g medium oatmeal
2 oz/50 g soft margarine
2 tablespoons skimmed milk
1 × 60 g bar plain carob, broken into pieces

NUTRITIONAL COMPARISON TABLE

	Carob Digestives	Chocolate Digestives
CALORIES	1304	1180
CARBOHYDRATE	170	140
FAT	66	61
PROTEIN	24	19
FIBRE	13	9
SODIUM	692	3227
POTASSIUM	815	778
IRON	10	7
CAFFEINE	—	0·03
THEOBROMINE	—	0·175

Lightly oil a baking sheet and set the oven to 350°F/180°C/Gas 4.

Sieve together the flour and baking powder and place in a bowl. Stir in the sugar and oatmeal and rub in the margarine as if you were making pastry – working as lightly as possible. Bind with half the milk and work to a soft dough in the bowl before rolling out on a lightly floured board to a thickness of about ¼ in (6 mm). Using a 3-in (7.5-cm) plain round biscuit cutter cut out the biscuits and transfer them to the baking sheet. Prick well with a fork and bake for 15 minutes. Remove from the oven and cool on a wire cooling tray.

When the biscuits are cold, melt the carob in the top of a double boiler or in a basin standing in a pan of hot water. Stir in the remaining milk. Using a palette knife, spread the top of the biscuits with the melted carob. Just before it sets make patterns in it with a fork or knife, if liked. Allow to become cold before storing in an airtight tin.

The Classics

Carob Ice-cream

SERVES 4

½ pint/300 ml skimmed milk
2 free-range eggs
1 tablespoon fructose
1 × 60 g bar plain carob, broken into pieces
4 oz/100 g quark

Place the milk in a saucepan or double boiler and heat until just below boiling point. Remove from the heat. Whisk the eggs and fructose together and pour the milk onto them, whisking all the time. Return to a clean pan through a sieve, and stir over the heat until the custard thickens. Do not allow the mixture to boil or it will curdle. When thickened remove from the heat and allow to cool.

Melt the carob pieces by placing in the top of a double boiler or in a basin standing in a pan of hot water. Blend it with the quark, then blend in the cooled custard. Make the ice-cream in your usual way (see pages 98–9).

NUTRITIONAL COMPARISON TABLE		
	Carob Ice-Cream	*Chocolate Ice-Cream*
CALORIES	742	1737
CARBOHYDRATE	68	124
FAT	36	127
PROTEIN	38	29·2
FIBRE	0·3	—
SODIUM	775	342
POTASSIUM	640	849
IRON	6	5
CAFFEINE	—	0·045
THEOBROMINE	—	0·26

The Classics

Carob Eclairs

MAKES 12

¼ pint/150 ml water
2 oz/50 g unsalted butter
3 oz/75 g 81% wholemeal flour
2 free-range eggs, lightly beaten

filling
½ oz/12 g gelatine
4 tablespoons boiling water
8 oz/225 g strained Greek yoghurt
1 free-range egg white

topping
1 × 60 g bar no-added-sugar plain carob, broken into pieces
2 tablespoons skimmed milk

Lightly oil a baking tray (or an éclair tray), and set oven to 400°F/200°C/ Gas 6. Fit a ½-inch/10-mm plain nozzle to a piping bag.

Place the water and butter in a saucepan and bring to the boil. Remove from the heat and stir until the butter has melted. Sieve the flour twice, and beat vigorously into the butter until the mixture forms a thick paste and leaves the sides of the pan in one shiny lump. Leave to cool for 3 minutes then gradually beat in the eggs, a little at a time, working the mixture well between additions. Do not let the paste become too soft because it must hold its shape when piped: omit a little egg, if necessary. Place the paste in

NUTRITIONAL COMPARISON TABLE		
	Carob Eclairs	*Chocolate Eclairs*
CALORIES	1464	2839
CARBOHYDRATE	100	241
FAT	95	196
PROTEIN	74	36
FIBRE	8	3
SODIUM	559	1057
POTASSIUM	1228	849
IRON	10	10
CAFFEINE	—	0·03
THEOBROMINE	—	0·175

The Classics

the piping bag and pipe 3½-inch/9-cm fingers of paste, keeping them quite thick, onto the prepared baking sheet (or into the moulded shapes of an éclair tray). Bake for 15 minutes then reduce the heat to 350°F/180°C/Gas 4 for a further 10 minutes.

Remove from the oven and make a split in the sides. Allow to dry out completely before filling.

To make the filling, sprinkle the gelatine onto the water and stir until dissolved. Leave to cool and, when on the point of setting, stir into the yoghurt. Whip the egg white until stiff and fold in. Chill before using to fill the éclairs.

For the topping, melt the carob bar in the top of a double boiler or in a basin standing in a pan of hot water, and mix in the milk. Spread the tops of the éclairs with this, then chill before serving.

The Classics

Carob Chip Cookies

MAKES 30

4 oz/100 g soft margarine
4 tablespoons clear honey
1 free-range egg
3 oz/75 g chopped walnuts
1½ oz/40 g sunflower seeds, lightly toasted
1 × 60 g bar no-added-sugar plain carob, finely chopped
6 oz/175 g wholemeal flour
1 teaspoon salt-free baking powder

NUTRITIONAL COMPARISON TABLE		
	Carob Chip Cookies	*Chocolate Chip Cookies*
CALORIES	2499	3385
CARBOHYDRATE	213	420
FAT	294	357
PROTEIN	51	45
FIBRE	19	9
SODIUM	1469	3697
POTASSIUM	1943	1695
IRON	13	10
CAFFEINE	—	0·0175
THEOBROMINE	—	0·1225

Lightly oil 2 baking trays and set the oven to 375°F/190°C/Gas 5.

Cream the margarine and honey until light and fluffy. Beat in the egg and fold in the nuts and sunflower seeds, together with the chopped carob bar. Sieve the flour together with the baking powder and fold into the mixture.

Place spoonfuls of mixture on the baking trays leaving plenty of space between them as they will spread. Bake for 15 minutes until golden brown. Remove and allow to cool on a wire cooling tray.

The Classics

Home-baking never looked better than with Carob Chip Cookies, page 32

Carob Mousse, page 33, is certainly a valuable work of art

Carob Mousse

SERVES 4

2 free-range eggs, separated
2 tablespoons clear honey
½ pint/300 ml skimmed milk
½ oz/12 g gelatine
4 tablespoons boiling water
2 × 60 g bars no-added-sugar plain carob
8 oz/225 g skimmed-milk soft cheese
decoration

carob shapes (p. 96) *or* soft fruit
Chantilly piping cream (optional, p. 22–3)

Place the egg yolks and honey in a bowl and whisk together. Heat the milk in a saucepan or double boiler until just below boiling point. Remove from the heat and pour onto the egg yolks and honey, stirring all the time. Return to a clean pan through a sieve and stir over a moderate heat until the custard thickens. Remove from heat and cool. Sprinkle the gelatine onto the water and stir to dissolve. Leave this to cool as well.

Melt the carob bars in the top of a double boiler or in a bowl over hot water. Stir into the cheese, then blend in the cooled custard. Stir in the cooled gelatine. Whisk the egg whites until stiff and when the custard is on the point of setting fold the whites into it and pour into a size 2 soufflé dish or individual ramekins. Chill to set.

Just before serving garnish with carob shapes or soft fruit, if in season, or other fresh fruit of choice and, if liked, pipe on Chantilly piping cream.

NUTRITIONAL COMPARISON TABLE		
	Carob Mousse	*Chocolate Mousse*
CALORIES	1206	1375
CARBOHYDRATE	104	67
FAT	54	106
PROTEIN	80	41
FIBRE	1	—
SODIUM	1482	322
POTASSIUM	1428	671
IRON	13	6·68
CAFFEINE	—	0·06
THEOBROMINE	—	0·35

The Classics

If you are used to baking with white flour, block margarines and white sugar, you will find these recipes quite a revelation. They demonstrate that there *are* cakes after wholemeal flour and that they can be every bit as delicious. In fact, as you get used to their new 'richness' of flavour without 'richness' of fat and sugar, you'll find that you come to regard the all-white versions as far from all right.

You will also notice some differences in the finished results. Because of its fibre content, wholemeal flour cannot produce cakes as light and fluffy as white flour, so don't think you have failed as a cook if the cakes do not rise as much as your old recipes used to – they make up for it in flavour.

Wholemeal flour (100%) is used in all the cake recipes, but you can introduce more air and lightness by sieving it well (twice instead of the usual once). Don't throw away the bran in the sieve – return it to the flour. Sieve the carob powder and cream or beat the mixtures well to introduce more air.

Cakes

Coffee and Walnut Gâteau

SERVES 10

4 oz/100 g soft margarine
3 oz/75 g light muscovado sugar
2 free-range eggs
4 oz/100 g wholemeal flour, sieved
1 tablespoon decaffeinated instant coffee, dissolved in
1 tablespoon water
2 oz/50 g walnut pieces

Topping
1 quantity Carob Frosting (p. 77)
½ × 60 g bar plain carob, grated

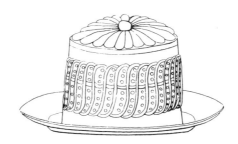

Lightly oil an 8-in (20-cm) cake tin and set the oven to 350°F/180°C/Gas 4.
   Cream together the margarine and sugar until pale and soft in consistency. Lightly beat the eggs and beat into the margarine and sugar mixture, adding a little flour if the mixture begins to curdle. Beat in the coffee and fold in the flour and nuts. Place in the prepared tin and bake for 30 minutes on the top shelf.
   When cooked remove from the oven and allow to become completely cold before cutting in half, horizontally, and sandwiching together with some of the frosting. Spread the remainder around the sides of the gâteau and the top. Press the grated carob into the sides of the gâteau (easily done by placing the gâteau on an icing turntable if you have one). Refrigerate until served.

Cakes

Carob Chip Cake

SERVES 8

3 oz/75 g wholemeal flour, sieved
3 oz/75 g wholemeal semolina
1 teaspoon salt-free baking powder
4 oz/100 g soft margarine
2 oz/50 g fructose
2 free-range eggs, separated
1 × 60 g bar no-added-sugar plain carob, finely chopped
1 tablespoon milk

Lightly oil an 8-in (20-cm) cake tin, and set the oven to 350°F/180°C/Gas 4.

Mix together the sieved flour, semolina and baking powder. Cream together the margarine, fructose and egg yolks until soft and pale. Fold in the finely chopped carob bar and the milk to give a soft consistency. Whisk the egg whites until firm and stiff and, using a metal tablespoon, fold into the mixture. Place in the prepared tin and bake for 25 minutes.

Remove from the oven and leave to cool on a wire cooling tray before storing in an airtight tin.

Carob Brioche

CUTS INTO 12 SLICES

8 oz/225 g wholemeal flour
1 × 60 g bar plain carob, finely chopped
½ oz/12 g fresh yeast
2 tablespoons water
2 free-range eggs, lightly beaten
2 oz/50 g soft margarine, melted

Lightly oil a large brioche mould, and set the oven to 425°F/220°C/Gas 7.

Sieve the flour into a mixing bowl and stir in the carob pieces. Cream the yeast and water with the eggs and margarine and add to the flour. Beat slightly until the mixture leaves the sides of the bowl cleanly. Knead lightly for 5 minutes and shape the dough into a round. Place in the mould.

Cover and leave to rise in a warm place for about an hour, or until just below the top of the mould. Bake for 15–20 minutes. Cool on a wire tray before removing from mould, then slice as required.

Individual brioche moulds are also available, and these make a nice breakfast dish served warm. This mixture will fill about 12 moulds.

Cakes

Lemon Sponge

SERVES 8–10

4 oz/100 g soft margarine
3 oz/75 g fructose
2 free-range eggs
6 oz/175 g wholemeal flour
zest and juice of ½ lemon
2 drops of lemon oil

carob filling

1 × 60 g bar no-added-sugar plain carob, broken into pieces
2 tablespoons clear honey
8 oz/225 g strained Greek yoghurt

Lightly oil 2 Victoria sponge sandwich tins, and set the oven to 350°F/ 180°C/Gas 4.

Cream together the margarine and fructose until pale and fluffy in consistency. Lightly beat the eggs and gradually beat into the mixture. Sieve the flour and fold in together with the lemon zest, juice and oil. Place in the prepared tins and bake for 30–35 minutes. When cooked cool on a wire cooling tray.

To make the filling, melt the carob by placing in the top of a double boiler or in a basin standing in a pan of hot water. Remove from heat, add the honey and carefully add a little at a time to the yoghurt, stirring well.

Sandwich the lemon sponges together with this.

Mocha Ring

SERVES 8–10

If liked, decorate with frosting and carob, or serve as a simple ring. The white frosting makes an attractive finish to the cake, especially when topped with zig-zags of melted carob.

3 free-range eggs
3 oz/75 g clear honey
1 × 60 g bar no-added-sugar plain carob, broken into pieces
1 tablespoon decaffeinated coffee granules
2 tablespoons water
3 oz/75 g wholemeal flour
1 dessertspoon decaffeinated ground coffee (filter fine)

frosting (optional, see above)

6 oz/175 g cottage cheese (sieved) *or* low-fat curd cheese
4 drops natural vanilla essence
3 oz/75 g strained Greek yoghurt
1 teaspoon clear honey
½ × 60 g bar no-added-sugar plain carob, broken into pieces

Lightly oil a savarin cake tin or Pyrex ring mould, and set the oven to 375°F/190°C/Gas 5.

Whisk together the eggs and honey in an electric mixer until thick and ropy, or whisk by hand in a basin over a pan of hot water. Place the carob pieces in the top of a double boiler or in a basin standing in a pan of hot water and add the instant coffee and the water. Melt, then whisk into the egg mixture. Sieve the flour well and fold into the cake mixture with the coffee grounds. Pour into the prepared tin or mould and bake for 25 minutes. Take out of the oven and cool a little before removing from the tin.

Blend the cheese with the remaining ingredients, except for the carob. Spread over the cooled ring. Melt the carob in a basin with a couple of tablespoons of water and pipe zig-zags of carob over the top of the frosting.

Cakes

Sarah's Carob Cake

SERVES 8

4 oz/100 g wholemeal flour
2 oz/50 g carob powder
2 teaspoons salt-free baking powder
6 oz/175 g soft margarine
4 oz/100 g muscovado sugar
2 tablespoons clear honey
3 free-range eggs
2 tablespoons milk

filling
4 oz/100 g low-fat soft cheese
juice of ½ lemon
1 small banana

topping
1 × 60 g bar plain carob, broken into pieces
a knob of butter *or* soft margarine
walnut halves

Lightly oil 2 × 7-in (17.5-cm) sandwich tins, and set the oven to 350°F/ 180°C/Gas 4.

Sieve together the flour, carob and baking powders. Cream together the margarine, sugar and honey until light and fluffy. Beat one egg in at a time to the latter mixture, beating well between each addition. Fold in the sieved flour and carob with a metal spoon. Stir in the milk to mix to a soft dropping consistency. Divide the mixture between the tins and lightly level the tops. Place in the centre of the oven and bake for 35–40 minutes until well risen and springy to the touch. Place the tins on a wire tray to cool before turning out the cakes and leaving to cool completely.

For the filling, mix the soft cheese with the lemon juice. Peel the banana and chop well, then mash with a fork into the cheese and spread evenly on one of the cakes. Melt the carob bar for the topping in the top of a double boiler or in a basin standing in a pan of hot water. Add the fat and beat until smooth and glossy. Using a palette knife, spread the topping over the top of the second cake until smooth. Decorate with walnut halves. When set, place carob-topped cake on top of filling-topped cake.

Cakes

Bavarian Carob Cake

SERVES 8

2 × 60 g bars no-added-sugar plain carob, broken into pieces
2 tablespoons skimmed milk
6 oz/175 g soft margarine
4 oz/100 g fructose
3 free-range eggs
4 oz/100 g wholemeal flour, sieved
Chantilly cream

8 oz/225 g strained Greek yoghurt
2 drops of natural vanilla essence
1 free-range egg white
to assemble

no-added-sugar black cherry jam
1 × 60 g bar plain carob, grated

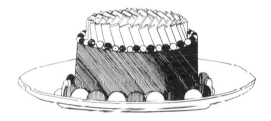

Lightly oil a 7–8-in (17.5–20-cm) cake tin, preferably with a loose bottom, and set the oven to 400°F/200°C/Gas 6.

Place the carob pieces and milk in the top of a double boiler or in a basin standing in a pan of hot water and melt, mixing well. Beat the margarine and fructose together until light and fluffy, and then beat in the eggs, one at a time. Remove the carob from the heat and beat into the mixture. Fold in the flour. Pour into the prepared tin and smooth the top. Bake for 30 minutes and cool on a wire tray.

To make the Chantilly Cream, place the yoghurt in a mixing bowl, and stir in the vanilla essence. Whisk the egg white until stiff. Lighten the yoghurt by folding in 2 tablespoons of the whisked egg white, then fold in the remaining egg white. Chill before use.

To assemble, cut the cold cake either in half or into 3 layers, and use the Chantilly Cream and jam to fill it. Decorate with more cream spread across the top of the cake and the grated carob around the edges.

Cakes

Carrot Cake

SERVES 10

4 oz/100 g soft margarine
4 oz/100 g light muscovado sugar
2 free-range eggs
8 oz/225 g wholemeal flour
1 teaspoon salt-free baking powder
½ teaspoon ground cinnamon
5 oz/150 g natural yoghurt
12 oz/325 g carrots, grated
1 × 60 g bar plain carob, finely diced

banana frosting

1 ripe banana, about 6 oz/175 g
juice of ½ lemon
4 oz/100 g low-fat cream *or* curd cheese

Lightly oil a 7-in (17.5-cm) square cake tin, and set the oven to 350°F/180°C/ Gas 4.

Cream together the margarine and sugar until light and fluffy, then add the eggs one at a time, beating well between additions. Sieve together the flour, baking powder and cinnamon, and fold into the mixture. Add the yoghurt and mix well. Fold in the carrots and carob and turn into the prepared tin. Bake for 55–60 minutes until an inserted skewer comes out clean.

To make the banana frosting, roughly mash the banana with the lemon juice. Place in a blender or a bowl and blend to a smooth purée with the cheese.

Cakes

Carob and Almond Log

SERVES 10

4 oz/100 g soft margarine
2 oz/50 g fructose
2 free-range eggs
4 oz/100 g ground almonds
1 × 60 g bar no-added-sugar plain carob, broken into pieces
2 oz/50 g wholemeal flour
2 tablespoons carob powder
2 teaspoons salt-free baking powder
1 teaspoon ground cinnamon

chestnut frosting (or carob cream, p. 53)

8 oz/225 g chestnut purée
2 fl. oz/60 ml milk
4 oz/100 g strained Greek yoghurt

Lightly oil a log tin, 8 in (20 cm) long by 2 in (5 cm) deep, and set the oven to 350°F/180°C/Gas 4.

Cream together the margarine and fructose until light and fluffy. Beat in the eggs and then fold in the ground almonds. Melt the carob pieces in the top of a double boiler or in a basin in a pan of hot water. Allow to cool slightly and stir into the egg mixture. Sieve together the flour, carob powder, baking powder and cinnamon, and fold into the mixture. Turn into the prepared tin and smooth the top. Bake for 40 minutes. Remove from the oven and cool slightly on a wire tray before removing from the tin. Leave to get completely cold.

To make the frosting, simply blend all the ingredients together. Smooth over the log with a palette knife, and dust top, if liked, with extra carob powder. Chill before serving or storing.

Cakes

Gooey Brownies

MAKES 9

4 oz/100 g wholemeal flour
2 tablespoons carob powder
1 teaspoon salt-free baking powder
3 oz/75 g light muscovado sugar
4 oz/100 g walnut pieces
2 oz/50 g soft margarine
1/8 pint/75 ml hot water
1/4 pint/150 ml skimmed milk

Lightly oil a 9-in (22.5-cm) square baking tin, and set the oven to 300°F/150°C/Gas 2.

Sieve the flour, carob powder and baking powder into a bowl, and stir in the sugar and nuts. Melt the margarine in a saucepan over a moderate heat and pour onto the dry ingredients. Stir well then add the hot water and milk. Pour the batter into the prepared tin, and bake for 40 minutes. Remove and allow to cool before cutting into squares and removing from the tin.

NB Do not use a loose-bottomed tin for this cake because the batter is very liquid, and you will have a messy oven to clean if you do.

Orange and Carob Marble Loaf

SERVES 8

4 oz/100 g soft margarine
3 oz/75 g light muscovado sugar
2 free-range eggs
4 oz/100 g wholemeal flour, sieved
1 oz/25 g carob powder mixed with 2 tablespoons water
zest of 1 orange
2 drops of orange oil

Lightly oil a small 1-lb (450-g) loaf tin, and set the oven to 325°F/160°C/Gas 3.

Cream together the margarine and sugar until light and fluffy. Beat in the eggs, then fold in the flour. Divide the cake mixture in half. To one-half, add the carob paste and mix in thoroughly. To the other half, add the zest of the orange and the orange oil and mix in well. Spoon alternatively into the prepared tin and swirl the mixtures together to achieve a marbled effect. Bake for 45–50 minutes until an inserted skewer comes out clean.

Cool on a wire baking tray and when cold store in an airtight tin.

Cakes

Carob Banana Cake

SERVES 8–10

3 oz/75 g soft margarine
3 oz/75 g light muscovado sugar
2 free-range eggs
1 ripe banana
6 oz/175 g wholemeal flour
1 oz/25 g carob powder
1 teaspoon salt-free baking powder
½ teaspoon mixed spice

Lightly oil a 7-in (17.5-cm) cake tin and set the oven to 350°F/180°C/Gas 4.

Cream together the margarine and sugar until pale and fluffy. Lightly beat the eggs and beat into the mixture one at a time, beating well between additions. Mash the banana with a fork and blend into the cake mixture. Sieve together the flour, carob powder, baking powder and spice and fold into the cake mixture. Spoon into the prepared tin and smooth the top. Bake for 45 minutes and allow to cool a little before removing from the tin.

Serve just as it is or decorate the top with sliced banana and halved grapes around the edge with a light dusting of extra carob powder in the centre.

Cakes

Swiss Roll

SERVES 6–8

The roll can be filled with jam alone, or with jam and
thick, strained Greek yoghurt. If filling with jam do this
when the roll is still hot, just before rolling up, but if
using yoghurt and jam then roll up with paper inside and
unroll and fill just before serving, or when the roll is
cold.

3 free-range eggs
3 oz/75 g clear honey
2½ oz/65 g wholemeal flour
1 oz/25 g carob powder
1 tablespoon boiling water

Lightly oil and line a Swiss roll tin with greaseproof paper. Oil the inside of
the paper too, and set the oven to 425°F/220°C/Gas 7.

Whisk the eggs and honey together with an electric beater – or by hand in
a basin standing over a pan of hot water – until it has increased in volume, is
thick and ropy in consistency, and pale in colour. Sieve the flour and carob
powder together and fold into the whisked mixture together with the
water. Pour into the prepared tin. Bake for 10–12 minutes until firm and
springy to the touch.

Place a sheet of greaseproof paper on a flat work surface and when the
cake is cooked invert it onto the paper. Carefully peel off the paper in which
the roll cooked and, using a sharp knife, trim the edges. If using jam spread
to within ½ in (12 mm) of the edges, and roll up at once from the short side,
making the first turn firm, then rolling lightly. If a yoghurt filling is to be
used, then roll up after trimming, with the new, clean piece of greaseproof
paper inside. When cold unroll carefully and fill.

Cakes

Passion Cake

SERVES 10

12 oz/325 g carrots, scrubbed
4 oz/100 g light muscovado sugar
2 tablespoons clear honey
8 oz/225 g soft margarine
3 free-range eggs
8 oz/225 g wholemeal flour, sieved
1½ teaspoons salt-free baking powder
1 tablespoon lemon juice
4 oz/100 g walnut pieces

frosting

8 oz/225 g low-fat cream cheese
2 dessertspoons clear honey
1 tablespoon carob powder
2 tablespoons water

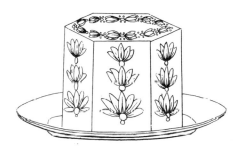

Lightly oil a loose-bottomed 8-in (20-cm) cake tin, and set the oven to 350°F/180°C/Gas 4.

Grate the carrots and place to one side. Cream together the sugar, honey and margarine until soft and light. Lightly beat the eggs and gradually add to the mixture, adding a little of the flour and baking powder – which have been sieved together – if the mixture curdles. Fold in the rest of the flour. Add the lemon juice and walnut pieces and place in the prepared tin. Bake for an hour. If the cake shows signs of over-browning, protect the top with a layer of greaseproof paper for the last 15 minutes. Remove and allow to cool on a wire cooling tray.

To make the frosting, cream together the cheese and honey. Blend the carob powder with the water to make a paste and add to the cheese. Spread this over the top of the cake when it is completely cold.

Cakes

Carob and Cinnamon Crumble Cake

SERVES 10

4 oz/100 g soft margarine
2 tablespoons clear honey
2 free-range eggs, lightly beaten
3½ oz/90 g wholemeal flour
½ oz/12 g carob powder
crumble

3 oz/75 g wholemeal flour
3 oz/75 g soft margarine
3 oz/75 g rolled oats
2 oz/50 g demerara sugar
1 tablespoon ground cinnamon

Lightly oil an 8-in (20-cm) cake tin, and set the oven to 375°F/190°C/Gas 5.

To make the cake, cream together the margarine and honey until light and fluffy. Gradually beat in the eggs, adding a little flour if the mixture begins to curdle. Fold in the flour and carob powder.

To make the crumble, sieve the flour into a mixing bowl and rub in the margarine until the mixture resembles breadcrumbs. Stir in the oats, sugar and cinnamon.

To assemble, place half the cake mixture in the base of the prepared tin, then sprinkle with half the crumble mixture. Layer on the rest of the sponge, levelling carefully with a spatula or knife, and top with the remaining crumble. Bake for 35–40 minutes. The cake is ready when an inserted skewer comes out clean. Remove from the oven and cool on a wire cooling tray. Store in an airtight tin.

Glossy eclairs, nice without the naughty with this low-calorie super light cream and silky carob topping, pages 30–1

Digestives are even more suggestive of another one when made with carob, page 28

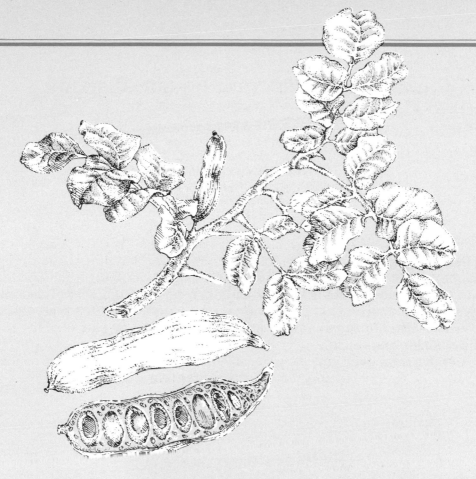

If we are trying to cut down on the fats in our diet, then high on the list of 'no nos' is probably biscuits, because they often contain large amounts of animal fats or hydrogenated vegetable fats. Hydrogenated fats have the same effect as saturated fats when they get into the body.

The highly refined nature of most biscuit ingredients also means that they are lacking in other valuable nutrients. Biscuits, however, are part of our social culture and we might still want to offer them to guests, or enjoy them as a family treat.

Making biscuits with high-quality unrefined ingredients, such as those used in these recipes – wholemeal flour, oats, nuts, dried fruits, soft vegetable magarine which is high in polyunsaturates, and carob in place of chocolate – will result in a much more nutritious biscuit for treats and special occasions.

Biscuits

Carob and Hazelnut Square Biscuits

MAKES 14

2 oz/50 g soft margarine
2 oz/50 g muscovado sugar
1 free-range egg, beaten
4 oz/100 g wholemeal flour
1 teaspoon baking powder
1 dessertspoon carob powder
2 oz/50 g chopped hazelnuts

Lightly oil a large baking tray, and set the oven to 350°F/180°C/Gas 4.

Beat together the margarine and sugar until light and fluffy. Add the egg and beat well. Sieve the flour, baking powder and carob together, and fold into the mixture, together with the nuts, to form a soft dough. Roll out on a lightly floured surface to ⅛-in (3-mm) thickness, and cut into squares using a biscuit cutter or square ravioli cutter. Place on the prepared baking tray and bake for 20 minutes.

Remove from oven and leave to cool and become crisp on a wire cooling tray. Store in an airtight tin.

Refrigerator Cookies

MAKES 16

3 oz/75 g soft margarine
2 oz/50 g muscovado sugar
3½ oz/90 g wholemeal flour
2 tablespoons carob powder
1 free-range egg
a few pinches of ground cinnamon

Lightly oil a large baking tray, and set the oven to 375°F/190°C/Gas 5.

Cream together the margarine and sugar until soft and pale. Sieve the flour and carob powder together. Beat the egg into the margarine mixture and then fold in the flour. Roll into a sausage shape of 3 in (7.5 cm) in diameter, and wrap in greaseproof paper. Chill the dough in the fridge for a minimum of 2 hours or place in the freezer for 30–40 minutes until it is firm. Slice thin cookies from the dough and place on the baking tray. Bake for 10 minutes.

Remove from oven and allow to cool on a wire cooling tray. Sprinkle the tops lightly with cinnamon just before serving.

Biscuits

Ginger Sponge Fingers

MAKES 18

3 oz/75 g soft margarine
2 oz/50 g fructose
3½ oz/90 g wholemeal flour
1½ teaspoons ground ginger
½ teaspoon ground cinnamon
2 free-range egg whites
1¼ × 60 g bars plain carob, broken into pieces

Lightly oil 2 baking trays and set the oven to 375°F/190°C/Gas 5.

Cream the margarine and fructose until soft and pale. Beat in the sieved flour and spices. In another bowl whisk the egg whites until firm. Fold 2 tablespoons of white into the flour mixture to lighten it, then fold in the remainder. Place the mixture into a piping bag with a ½-in (12-mm) plain nozzle, and pipe 18 finger biscuits, leaving generous space between them because they will spread. Bake for 15 minutes. Remove and allow to cool on a wire cooling tray.

While the biscuits are cooling melt the carob in the top of a double boiler, or in a basin standing in a pan of hot water. Using a palette knife spread the carob over the base of the ginger fingers when they are cold, and place them upside down on the cooling tray while the carob sets.

Hazelnut Hearts

MAKES 28

1 free-range egg white
3 oz/75 g fructose
1¼ × 60 g bar plain carob, grated
1½ oz/40 g wholemeal flour, sieved
2 oz/50 g ground hazelnuts
1 oz/25 g hazelnuts, finely chopped

Lightly oil 2 baking trays and set the oven to 375°F/190°C/Gas 5.

Whisk the egg white until firm, then fold in the fructose, grated carob, flour and nuts to form a dough. Turn onto a lightly floured surface and roll out to about ¼-in (6-mm) thickness. Using a small cutter cut out heart-shaped biscuits and lift onto the prepared baking sheet. Bake for 15–18 minutes.

Remove and cool on a wire tray. Store in an airtight container.

Biscuits

Carob Oaties

MAKES 8

2 oz/50 g clear honey
2 oz/50 g soft margarine
2 oz/50 g light muscovado sugar
¾ × 60 g bar no-added-sugar carob, broken into pieces
2 oz/50 g wholemeal flour
1½ oz/40 g rolled oats

Lightly oil a baking tray and heat the oven to 350°F/180°C/Gas 4.
  Place the honey, margarine, sugar and carob pieces in a saucepan over a gentle heat and stir until melted. Remove from the heat and stir in the flour and oats. Place 8 dessertspoons on the prepared baking sheet and flatten with the back of the spoon. Bake for 15 minutes, then remove from oven. Place on a wire cooling tray to cool and crisp. Store in an airtight tin.

Carob Squares

MAKES 9

6 oz/175 g wholemeal flour
4 oz/100 g medium oatmeal
4 oz/100 g soft margarine
2 oz/50 g light muscovado sugar
1 oz/25 g hazelnuts, chopped
4 tablespoons skimmed milk
1 oz/25 g carob powder

Lightly oil an 8-in (20-cm) square cake tin, and set the oven to 375°F/190°C/Gas 5.
  Sieve the flour into a mixing bowl and add the oatmeal. Cut the margarine into small pieces and rub into the flour and oatmeal until the mixture resembles breadcrumbs. Stir in the sugar and nuts. Halve the mixture. To one-half add 2 tablespoons of milk, and press that into the base of the prepared tin. To the other half add the carob powder, mix well, then add the remaining milk and press on top of the mixture already in the tin. Bake for 30 minutes.
  Remove from the oven and allow to cool slightly before cutting into squares. When cold remove from the tin and store in an airtight container.

Biscuits

Carob Shortbread

SERVES 8

6 oz/175 g wholemeal flour
4 oz/100 g unsalted butter
1½ oz/40 g fructose
1 level tablespoon carob powder

Lightly oil a baking sheet, and set the oven to 325°F/160°C/Gas 3.

Sieve the flour into a mixing bowl. Rub in the butter and stir in the fructose and carob. Press lightly to a soft dough and work lightly on a floured surface. Roll into a 6-in (15-cm) circle and lift onto the baking sheet. Pinch the edges or imprint the shortbread if you have a *wooden mould* to pattern it with. Bake for 35 minutes.

Remove and cool on a wire cooling tray. Cut into triangular slices.

Carob Cream Sandwiches

MAKES 10

4 oz/100 g soft margarine
2 oz/50 g muscovado sugar
4 oz/100 g wholemeal flour
2 tablespoons carob powder
1 dessertspoon decaffeinated coffee dissolved
in 1 dessertspoon hot water

cream filling

1 tablespoon carob powder
4 oz/100 g quark *or* similar low-fat soft white cheese

Lightly oil a baking tray, and set the oven to 375°F/190°C/Gas 5.

Cream together the margarine and sugar until light and fluffy. Sieve the flour and carob powder together, and add to the creamed mixture with the coffee to make a soft paste. With floured hands lightly roll out 20 walnut-sized pieces of paste and place on the baking tray. Press down with the back of a fork dipped in hot water. Bake for 12 minutes. Remove, and when slightly cool, transfer to a wire cooling tray.

To make the cream filling, simply combine the ingredients. Do not sandwich them together, though, until just before serving or else the biscuits will absorb the moisture from the filling and go soft.

Biscuits

Carob Chequerboards

MAKES 12

These are enjoyable to make but a little time-consuming, so only attempt if you are in the mood for baking! They are a nice, short biscuit and well worth the effort which can be a lot of fun.

6 oz/175 g soft margarine
2 oz/50 g fructose
8 oz/225 g wholemeal flour, sieved
1 tablespoon carob powder
1 tablespoon cold water
a few drops of natural vanilla essence

Lightly oil a large baking tray and, towards the end of chilling the mixture, set the oven to 375°F/190°C/Gas 5.

Beat the margarine, fructose and flour together to a dough, and remove one-third from the bowl. Mix together the carob and water to make a paste, and work into the dough in the bowl. Work the vanilla essence into the separate third of dough. Using half the carob dough and all of the vanilla dough, make 3 sausage shapes from each type of dough, each about 6 in (15 cm) long. Place 2 carob sausages on the board with a vanilla one in the middle and then place the remaining sausages on top to make the chequerboard effect.

Flour the board and roll the remaining carob dough to make a sheet large enough to wrap around the outside of the sausages; this is quite tricky, but the dough is soft and can be joined easily. Shape the wrapped sausages into an oblong, wrap in greaseproof paper, and leave to firm in the fridge for at least 2 hours (or in the freezer for 30 minutes) until thoroughly chilled. Remove and slice off 12 biscuits, placing them on the oiled baking tray.

Bake for 15 minutes. Remove and cool. Store in an airtight tin.

Ginger Biscuits

MAKES 16

2 oz/50 g wholemeal flour
1 teaspoon baking powder
1 teaspoon ground ginger
2 oz/50 g medium oatmeal
1 oz/25 g light muscovado sugar
2 oz/50 g soft margarine
2 tablespoons clear honey
1¼ × 60 g bars plain carob, broken into pieces

Lightly oil a baking tray, and set the oven to 375°F/190°C/Gas 5.

Sieve the flour, baking powder and ginger into a mixing bowl and stir in the oatmeal. Place the sugar, margarine and honey in a saucepan and melt over a gentle heat. Stir in the flour. Place generous teaspoonfuls on the prepared baking tray, leaving space between the biscuits to allow them to spread. Press the tops lightly with a hot fork to make indentations and flatten the biscuits. Bake for 15 minutes. Remove from oven and allow to cool on a wire cooling rack.

Melt the carob pieces in the top of a double boiler or in a basin standing in a pan of hot water. Spread the carob over either the base of the biscuits, or over half the biscuit (base and top), as preferred. Leave to set on the cooling tray before storing in an airtight tin.

Biscuits

Mint Thins

MAKES 22

2 oz/50 g soft margarine
2 oz/50 g light muscovado sugar
1 free-range egg
4 oz/100 g wholemeal flour, sieved
1 teaspoon peppermint essence
1 × 60 g bar no-added-sugar plain carob, broken into pieces

Lightly oil a small Swiss roll tin measuring 10 × 6 in (25 × 15 cm), and set the oven to 400°F/200°C/Gas 6.

Cream together the margarine and sugar until soft and pale. Beat in the egg and the flour, then add the peppermint essence. Spread the mixture over the base of the prepared tin, using a palette knife to smooth and flatten it. Bake for 20 minutes on the middle shelf then remove from the oven and allow to cool a little before turning out of the tin. Trim the edges and allow to cool further before cutting into fingers.

Before separating the fingers, though, melt the carob in the top of a double boiler or in a basin standing in a pan of hot water. Make a cone of greaseproof paper with a very narrow opening and spoon the melted carob into the cone. Then squeeze the carob through to drizzle over the biscuits in a zig-zag pattern. You will have to work quickly because the carob is hot and difficult to contain in the bag. Allow the carob to set before you pull the fingers apart, and serve or store them.

Biscuits

Moist and succulent Passion Cake, page 47, is upstaged by a bevy of
biscuits. *From the back:* Dumb-bells, page 57; Carob Chequerboards,
page 54; Mint Thins, page 56; and Ginger Biscuits, page 55

Smooth Carob Ice-Cream outside and fruity Strawberry Ice-Cream
inside this explosive bombe, page 100, and (*below*) a frozen
pineapple parfait tops a crunchy base for Pineapple Pie, page 85

Now you know why Black Forest Gâteau is Britain's favourite dessert, pages 20–1

Petits Fours, the perfect way to finish. *From the top:* De Luxe Truffles, some coated with carob powder, some shining through, page 60; Mint and Carob Chip Moulds, page 62; and Date Cups, cups of carob full of date and marzipan purée, page 61

Dumb-bells

MAKES 32 BISCUITS OR 16 DUMB-BELLS

3 free-range eggs, separated
3 oz/75 g light muscovado sugar
2 drops of natural vanilla essence
4 oz/100 g wholemeal flour, sieved

filling and coating

1 quantity carob cream (p. 53) *or* no-added-sugar jam
1 × 60 g bar plain carob, broken into pieces
½ oz/12 g soft margarine
2 tablespoons milk

Lightly oil a baking sheet, and set the oven to 375°F/190°C/Gas 5. Fit a piping bag with a ¼-in (6-mm) plain nozzle.

Whisk together the egg yolks and sugar until pale in colour and stiff in consistency. Add the vanilla essence. Whisk the egg whites until stiff and forming firm peaks. Fold half the whites into the egg and sugar mixture, then fold in the flour and the remaining whites. Place in the piping bag and pipe 2½-inch (6-cm) long biscuits onto the prepared tray. Bake for 15 minutes until crisp. Remove and cool on a wire tray.

When cold sandwich together with a little jam or Carob Cream. For the coating, place the carob pieces, margarine and milk in the top of a double boiler or in a basin standing in a pan of hot water, and melt. Dip each end of the dumb-bells into the carob and return to the cooling tray to set.

Biscuits

Home-made petits fours make a really special end to a dinner party. They are also delicious with coffee, if you have visitors at coffee-time, and make excellent gifts for birthdays and for Christmas.

Here we have a selection of easily made petits fours, many of which are not baked, but made by melting ingredients in a saucepan on the cooker top and mixing them before refrigerating to set – simple enough for children to help with (or make).

Arrange the petits fours in pretty paper cases and pack them in one of the very attractive gift boxes now available from stationers' or gift shops, or cover your own box with an original choice of gift-wrap paper for a super present.

Petits Fours

Almond Clusters

MAKES 12

2 oz/50 g flaked almonds
1 oz/25 g stem ginger
1 × 60 g bar plain carob, broken into pieces
1 tablespoon clear honey *or* syrup in which the ginger was preserved

Toast the flaked almonds lightly. Finely dice or grate the ginger. Melt the carob in the top of a double boiler, or in a basin standing in a pan of hot water. Remove from the heat and stir in the other ingredients.

When cool enough to handle form into 12 little mounds on a non-stick baking tray and leave to cool. When cold place in paper petits fours cases.

Walnut Clusters

MAKES 8

1 × 60 g bar no-added-sugar plain carob, broken into pieces
1 oz/25 g walnut pieces
2 oz/50 g raisins

Melt the carob in the top of a double boiler or in a basin standing in a pan of hot water. Remove from the heat and stir in the other ingredients.

When cool enough to handle form into 8 little mounds on a non-stick baking tray and leave until cold. Place in paper petits fours cases.

De Luxe Truffles

MAKES 10

1½ × 60 g bars no-added-sugar plain carob, broken into pieces
1 free-range egg yolk
½ oz/12 g unsalted butter
1 teaspoon Armagnac
1 teaspoon whole milk
a little carob powder

Melt the carob pieces in the top of a double boiler or in a basin standing in a pan of hot water. Remove from the heat and stir in the rest of the ingredients, except for the carob powder.

Chill until cool enough to handle (I find 10 minutes in the freezer cools the mixture sufficiently), then roll into little balls in the palm of your hand. Roll in the carob powder and place in the petits fours cases. Chill until served.

Petits Fours

Date Cups

MAKES 10

1 × 60 g bar plain carob, broken into pieces
2 oz/50 g cooking dates
2 oz/50 g marzipan
a few tablespoons cold water

Place 10 petits fours paper cases on a flat surface and have another 10 ready. Melt the carob in the top of a double boiler or in a basin standing in a pan of hot water. Place a teaspoonful of the carob in the base of a paper case and press in one of the spare cases to spread the carob up the sides of the case. Leave the paper case inside. Repeat with the other cases and chill in the fridge to set. When set remove the inside paper cases.

Meanwhile place the dates and marzipan in a saucepan with enough water to cook to a smooth purée without burning. Stir from time to time, breaking up the dates and marzipan with a wooden spoon. Remove and allow to cool. When the carob cases are set and the date purée cold fill the cases with the purée. Remove outer paper cases to reveal the carob cups.

Piped Petits Fours

MAKES 30

4 oz/100 g soft margarine
2 oz/50 g demerara sugar, ground to powder in a coffee mill
1 tablespoon carob powder
1 free-range egg
5 oz/150 g wholemeal flour

Lightly oil 2 baking sheets, and fit a piping bag with a star nozzle. Set the oven to 325°F/160°C/Gas 3.

Beat the margarine until it is soft, then add the remaining ingredients and beat to a soft paste. Place in the piping bag and pipe small stars onto the prepared baking sheet. Leave space between them because they will spread a little. Bake for 15 minutes. Allow to cool and become crisp on a wire cooling tray.

Petits Fours

Carob Macaroons

MAKES ABOUT 30

2–3 sheets of rice paper
2 free-range egg whites
4 oz/100 g ground almonds
1 tablespoon carob powder
4 oz/100 g fructose
30 almond pieces

Place the rice paper on 2 or 3 baking sheets, and fit a piping bag with a ½-in (12-mm) plain nozzle. Set the oven to 325°F/160°C/Gas 3.

Whisk the egg whites until firm and stiff. Fold in the ground almonds and carob powder. Add the fructose and whisk again. Place in the piping bag and pipe small mounds onto the rice paper. Top each with a piece of almond and bake for 25 minutes.

Remove and allow to cool before breaking away the excess rice paper and storing in an airtight tin.

Mint and Carob Chip Moulds

MAKES 24

For this you will need a set of metal petits fours moulds which are like tiny cake tins and come in different shapes.

3 oz/75 g soft margarine
1½ oz/40 g fructose
2 free-range egg yolks
4 oz/100 g wholemeal flour
a few drops of mint essence
½ × 60 g bar no-added-sugar plain carob, finely chopped

Lightly oil the petits fours moulds and place inside a Swiss roll tin to contain them in the oven. Set the oven to 350°F/180°C/Gas 4.

Beat together the margarine and fructose until light and fluffy. Cream in the egg yolks. Sieve the flour and then fold into the mixture. Add the mint essence, and fold in the carob. Place teaspoonfuls in the prepared moulds and bake for 20 minutes.

Take out of the oven and allow to cool in the tins before removing.

Petits Fours

The versatility of carob really comes to the fore when using it for pâtisserie items. Unlike chocolate, it does not have to be tempered and can be simply melted and used as a spread or dip to coat pâtisserie items.

With the addition of a little skimmed milk powder or liquid milk, carob attains a good gloss which it does not naturally have because it is free from cocoa butter, the substance that gives chocolate its sheen.

Carob makes a delicious filling for the irresistible French Pain au Chocolat or, in our case, Pain au Carob, made with wholemeal or granary flour.

So, put on your confectioner's apron and have a go at the more challenging recipes in this section which add a 'professional' touch to their presentation.

Pâtisserie

Swiss Buns

MAKES 8

These are very short in texture and can also make excellent petits fours by piping into petits fours cases: makes 24.

4 oz/100 g soft margarine
1 oz/25 g light muscovado sugar
3 oz/75 g wholemeal flour, sieved
1 oz/25 g carob powder
no-added-sugar jam

Place 8 paper cake cases on a baking tray, and set the oven to 350°F/180°C/Gas 4. Fit a piping bag with a rosette nozzle.

Beat together the margarine and sugar until light and fluffy. Beat in the sieved flour and carob powder to form a stiff paste. Place in the piping bag and pipe into the baking cases in a round leaving a little indentation, if possible, in the centre. Bake for 20 minutes.

Remove from the oven, and leave on a cooling tray. When cold place a tiny blob of jam in the centre of the buns – raspberry or blackcurrant is nice.

Japs

MAKES 12

2 free-range egg whites
3 oz/75 g fructose
2½ oz/65 g ground hazelnuts
1 oz/25 g wholemeal flour, sieved

coating

no-added-sugar jam *or* carob cream (p. 53)
desiccated coconut
carob powder

Lightly oil a baking tray and set the oven to 250°F/120°C/Gas ½. Fit a piping bag with a ½-in (12-mm) plain nozzle.

Whisk the egg whites until stiff and holding firm peaks, then whisk in half the fructose until smooth. Fold in the rest of the fructose, together with the ground nuts and sieved flour. Place in the piping bag and pipe into 12 rounds about 1 in (2.5 cm) high. Bake for an hour, or until dried out and browned.

Mask the sides with jam or Carob Cream, and roll in desiccated coconut. Dust the tops with carob powder.

Pâtisserie

Look through any French Pâtisserie window and you won't be able to
resist temptations like Marzipan Slices (*bottom shelf*), pages 70–1; Carob
Toscaners, page 72; and (*top shelf*), Carob Madeleines, page 69

Far lower in calories than conventional cheesecakes, these will also leave you as pretty as a picture. *From the top:* Orange Cheesecake, page 95; Peach and Carob Cheesecake, page 79; and a Pâtissier's delight, Carob Fruit Tart, pages 66–7

Viennese Fingers

MAKES 10

4 oz/100 g soft margarine
1 oz/25 g light muscovado sugar
4 oz/100 g wholemeal flour, sieved
2 drops of natural vanilla essence

coating
¾ × 60 g bar no-added-sugar plain carob, broken into pieces
1 oz/25 g soft margarine
1 tablespoon clear honey

Lightly oil a baking sheet and set the oven to 350°F/180°C/Gas 4. Fit a piping bag with a wide rosette nozzle.

Beat together the margarine and sugar until light and fluffy. Beat in the sieved flour and vanilla and place the paste in the piping bag. Pipe fingers of 2½–3 in (6–7.5 cm) in length onto the prepared baking tray, and bake for 20 minutes. Remove from oven and cool on a wire tray.

To make the coating, melt the carob pieces, margarine and honey together over a low heat, stirring to prevent sticking or burning. Allow to cool slightly before use. When the biscuits are quite cold dip each end of the fingers into the carob coating.

Coconut Castles

MAKES 12

1 sheet of rice paper
2 free-range egg whites
2 oz/50 g brown rice flour
2 oz/50 g fructose
4 oz/100 g desiccated coconut
2 teaspoons carob powder

Place the rice paper on a baking tray, and set the oven to 325°F/160°C/Gas 3.

Whisk the egg whites well until firm. Mix together all the remaining ingredients and fold them into the whites, using a metal tablespoon.

Gently mould the mixture into 12 little castles, placing them on the rice paper as you work. Rough the edges slightly using a couple of forks and bake in the bottom of the oven for 50 minutes. Remove and cool on a wire cooling tray.

Pâtisserie

Carob Fruit Tart

SERVES 6–8

This is a very 'professional' recipe so give yourself plenty of time. The tart is a pastry case filled with a sponge topped with custard and fresh fruit. Any fruit may be used, but choose contrasting colours for the most dramatic effect.

4 oz/100 g wholemeal flour, sieved
2 oz/50 g soft margarine
water to mix

sponge

2 oz/50 g soft margarine
2 oz/50 g light muscovado sugar
1 free-range egg
2 oz/50 g wholemeal flour, sieved
1 drop of natural vanilla essence

carob confectioner's custard

½ oz/12 g gelatine
4 tablespoons boiling water
3 free-range egg yolks
1 oz/25 g fructose
½ pint/300 ml skimmed milk
1 × 60 g bar no-added-sugar plain carob, broken into pieces

topping

a few black grapes
½ banana
lemon juice
½ peach or nectarine

to assemble

1¼ × 60 g bars plain carob, broken into pieces

Pâtisserie

Lightly oil an 8-in (20-cm) flan ring and an 8-in (20-cm) cake tin. Set oven to 375°F/190°C/Gas 5.

Make the pastry case first by rubbing together the flour and margarine until they resemble breadcrumbs. Add enough water to make a soft pastry. Roll out and line the flan ring, and inter-line with greaseproof paper weighted down with baking beans. Bake blind for 25 minutes. Take out of the oven, remove beans and paper, and allow to cool. Turn oven down to 350°F/180°C/Gas 4.

To make the sponge, cream together the margarine and sugar until light and fluffy, then beat in the egg and fold in the flour and vanilla essence. Place in the prepared cake tin and bake for 30 minutes. When cooked remove from oven and allow to cool.

To make the Carob Confectioner's Custard, sprinkle the gelatine onto the hot water and stir until dissolved (when the liquid becomes transparent). Leave on one side to cool. Whisk together the egg yolks, fructose and milk in a blender. Melt the carob in the top of a double boiler or in a basin standing in a pan of hot water. When melted, carefully pour into the milk, stirring all the time to keep the mixture smooth. Continue stirring over the heat for 5 minutes or so until the custard thickens. (At this point the mixture could be used as ordinary carob custard.) Remove from the heat and stir in the dissolved gelatine.

To assemble, have ready the pastry case, the sponge filling, the Carob Confectioner's Custard and the fruit topping. First melt the carob in the top of a double boiler or in a basin standing in a pan of hot water. When melted spread over the base of the pastry case and put the sponge on top. Pour the Confectioner's Custard over this and chill to set. Halve the grapes, slice the banana thinly (into the lemon juice to prevent browning), and slice the peach or nectarine without peeling it. When the custard has set arrange the fruit on top and serve.

Pâtisserie

Pear Frangipane

SERVES 4–6

The combination of pears and carob is a delicious one
that is enhanced here with the almondy soft sponge of
the frangipane.

2 pears, about 7 oz/200 g each
4 oz/100 g wholemeal flour
1 oz/25 g carob powder
4 oz/100 g soft margarine
water
2 oz/50 g light muscovado sugar
1 free-range egg
2 oz/50 g ground almonds

Lightly oil a crinkly edged, loose-bottomed flan tin – 5½ in (14 cm) wide by
2 in (5 cm) deep – and set the oven to 375°F/190°C/Gas 5.

Peel and core the pears, halve, and poach in a little water for 15 minutes.
Drain and place on one side to dry.

For the pastry, sieve 3 oz (75 g) of the flour into a mixing bowl with the
carob powder, then rub in half the margarine until the mixture resembles
breadcrumbs. Stir in a little water to make a soft dough and roll out on a
lightly floured board. Line the prepared tin and place on one side.

To make the sponge, beat together the remaining margarine and the
sugar until pale in colour and fluffy in consistency. Beat in the egg and then
fold in the remaining flour and the ground almonds.

Place the pear halves, core side downwards, in the base of the pastry-lined
flan tin, and spoon the sponge mixture over the top (the halved pears may
poke through a little). Bake for 30 minutes then remove from oven and
allow to cool before taking the side of the tin away. The frangipane can be
cut from the base of the tin. Best served slightly warm or cold.

Pâtisserie

Carob Madeleines

MAKES 6

1½ oz/40 g soft margarine
2½ oz/65 g wholemeal flour
½ oz/12 g carob powder
3 free-range eggs
3 oz/75 g fructose
½ tablespoon potato flour *or* cornflour
no-added-sugar jam
desiccated coconut

Oil 6 dariole moulds and stand them inside a Swiss roll tin, or other baking container, to keep them upright and together in the oven. Set the oven to 375°F/190°C/Gas 5.

Melt the margarine over a moderate heat in a saucepan. Sieve the flour into a mixing bowl together with the carob powder. Whisk together the eggs and fructose until pale in colour, and thick and ropy in consistency. Pour the melted margarine into the egg mixture and fold in together with the flours. Pour into the prepared moulds and bake for 15–20 minutes.

Remove from the oven and allow to cool slightly before easing away from the sides of the moulds by slipping a palette knife inside the tins. Invert and tap on the top to remove the cakes. Allow to cool slightly before spreading with jam, very thinly, and rolling in a plateful of desiccated coconut.

Pâtisserie

Marzipan Slices

MAKES 12

These are rather rich treats and quite time-consuming to make, so they are for the enthusiastic cook! Choose a marzipan without added colourings etc., often called White Marzipan on the pack, or a raw cane sugar marzipan from the health-food shop.

2 oz/50 g soft margarine
3 oz/75 g wholemeal flour
1 oz/25 g cornflour
3 free-range eggs
3 oz/75 g clear honey
2 × 8 oz/225 g bars marzipan
no-added-sugar apricot jam
¾ × 60 g bar no-added-sugar plain carob, broken into pieces
a little angelica for garnish, if liked

Line a 7-in (17.5-cm) square baking tin with greaseproof paper, and set the oven to 350°F/180°C/Gas 4.

Melt the margarine over a low heat then remove and cool. Sieve together the flour and cornflour. Whisk the eggs and honey in an electric mixer until thick and ropy in consistency: if you do not have an electric mixer use a hand whisk, placing the ingredients in a bowl over a pan of hot water, to speed the process. Carefully fold the melted margarine and flour into the egg mixture, and pour into the prepared tin. Bake for 30 minutes on the top shelf. When cooked, remove from the oven and allow to cool on a wire cooling tray. Peel off the paper and cut in half.

On a floured board roll the marzipan out very thinly. Cut off 2 large rectangles to fit the tops of the 2 halves. Brush the marzipan with jam and place on top of the cake. Then cut strips to fit around the sides of the 2 rectangles, brushing them with jam in the same way. Now cut the 2 halves each into 3 slices and place thin marzipan strips on the exposed sides. Now cut each slice into a triangle and repeat the marzipan strips until all the sides and the tops of the slices are covered with marzipan.

Melt the carob in the top of a double boiler or in a basin standing in a pan of hot water. Using a palette knife spread some of the carob on the slices to make different patterns on each. For example, on some you could spread the sides with carob, some the tops, some half the tops and sides. Cut diamonds of angelica and place on the non-carob-coated tops, if liked.

Pâtisserie

Marzipan Slices

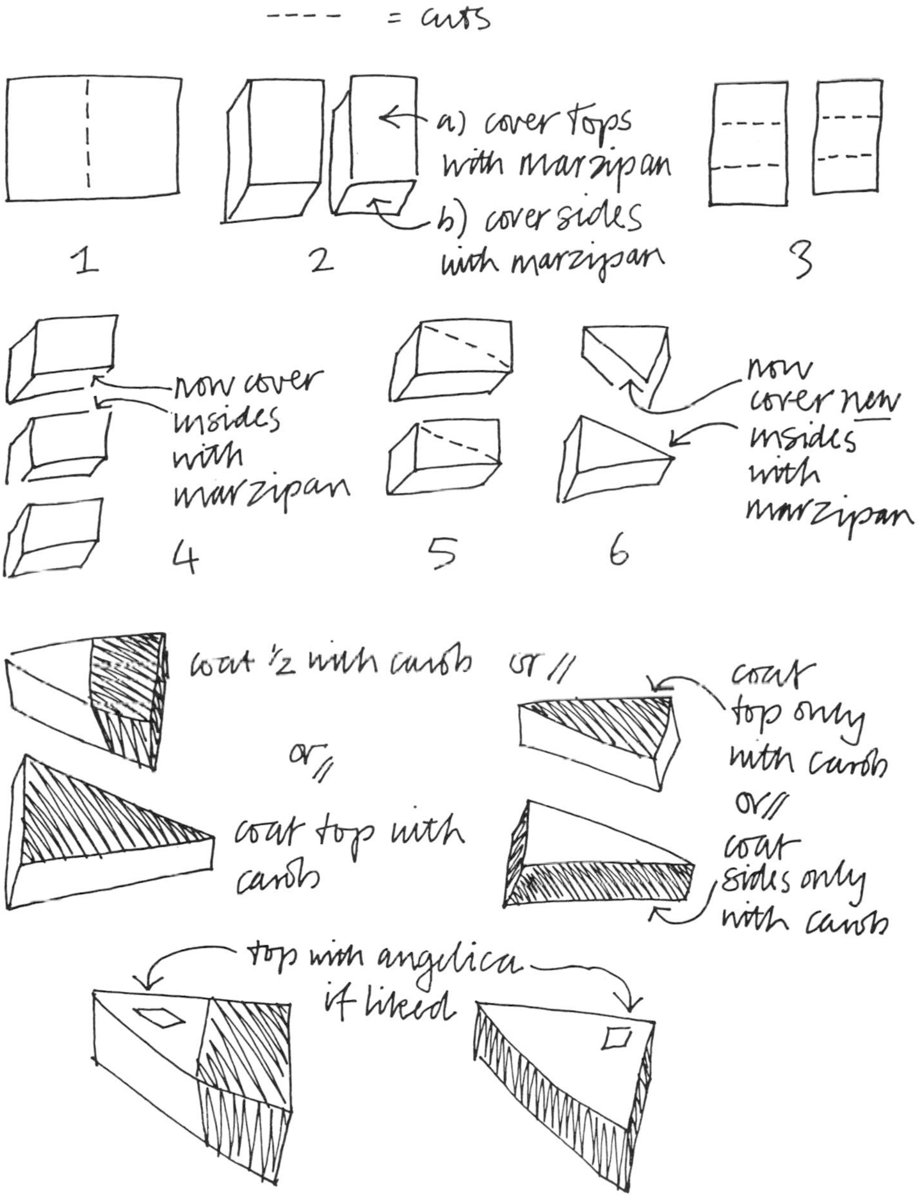

---- = cuts

1

2

a) cover tops with marzipan

b) cover sides with marzipan

3

4

now cover insides with marzipan

5

6

now cover new insides with marzipan

coat ½ with carob   or //

coat top only with carob

or //

or //

coat top with carob

coat sides only with carob

top with angelica if liked

Carob Toscaner

MAKES 9

Toscaner is a speciality at my local Swiss pâtisserie.
After tasting it, I thought I would create a wholefood
carob version and it is very near the original!

4 oz/100 g soft margarine
2 oz/50 g light muscovado sugar
2 free-range eggs
4 oz/100 g ground almonds
2 oz/50 g ground brown rice
2 drops of bitter almond essence
2 rounded tablespoons no-added-sugar apricot jam
1½ oz/40 g flaked almonds
2 × 60 g bars plain carob, broken into pieces

Lightly oil a 7½-in (19-cm) square baking tin and set the oven to 350°F/
180°C/Gas 4.

Cream together the margarine and sugar until light and soft in consistency. Lightly beat the eggs and add a little to the mixture at a time. Fold in the
almonds, ground rice and almond essence, and spread the mixture in the
base of the prepared tin. Spread the jam over the top and sprinkle on the
flaked almonds. Bake for 35 minutes on the middle shelf.

Take out of the oven and allow to cool before removing from the tin by
inverting onto a cooling tray. Slice into 9 squares.

Melt the carob in the top of a double boiler or in a basin standing in a pan
of hot water. Using a palette knife spread the carob first around the sides of
each square and then across the base. Leave inverted on the cooling tray
until the carob is set and cold. Store the slices in an airtight tin.

Pâtisserie

Easy Croissants

MAKES 16

This method is an all-in-one process rather than the long folding and turning process usually associated with croissants and flaky pastries. It has less fat and a softer, more bread-like consistency, but is delicious.

12 oz/325 g wholemeal *or* granary flour
6 oz/175 g unsalted butter
7 fl. oz/200 ml skimmed milk
½ oz/12 g fresh yeast, crumbled
½ oz/12 g clear honey
½ × 25 mg vitamin C tablet, crushed
egg or milk, to glaze
carob spread
1 × 60 g bar plain carob, broken into pieces
4 tablespoons water
1 oz/25 g flour
1 oz/25 g margarine

Lightly oil 2 baking sheets and set the oven to 425°F/220°C/Gas 7.

Place the flour in a mixing bowl, add the butter, and rub in until the texture is bigger than the breadcrumb consistency required for pastry. Mix together the milk, yeast, honey and vitamin C in a jug, and stir well. Pour into the flour and mix to a dough. Knead lightly for 5 minutes then divide the dough in half. Roll out each half on a lightly floured surface into a large circle, and cut each circle into 8 triangular segments.

To make the Carob Spread, melt the carob with the water in the top of a double boiler or in a basin standing in a pan of hot water, stirring to combine. In another pan mix together the flour and margarine to make a roux and cook, stirring, for 2 minutes. Gradually stir in the carob to make a thick spread.

Place a teaspoon of Carob Spread at the wide end of each triangle of dough and roll up from that wide end into a croissant shape. Place on the prepared baking sheet, cover and leave to double in size.

When risen, glaze with lightly beaten egg, or milk, and bake for 20 minutes. Remove from oven and cool on a wire cooling tray.

Pâtisserie

Pain au Carob

MAKES 16 ROLLS

1 lb/450 g wholemeal flour
1½ oz/40 g walnuts, finely chopped
½ pint/300 ml skimmed milk
1 oz/25 g light muscovado sugar
2 oz/50 g soft margarine
¾ oz/18 g fresh yeast, crumbled
1 × 25 mg vitamin C tablet, crushed to powder
1 × 60 g bar plain carob *or* 1 quantity Carob Spread (p. 73)
egg or milk, to glaze

Lightly oil 2 baking sheets and set the oven to 425°F/220°C/Gas 7.

Sieve the flour into a mixing bowl and stir in the nuts. Warm the milk to 98°F/36°C, remove from heat and stir in the sugar, margarine, yeast and vitamin C. Pour onto the flour and mix to a dough. Knead lightly for 3 minutes then leave to rest, covered in a bowl, until doubled in size.

Place on a floured surface and knead again. Cut into 16 pieces of equal size. At this stage you can either pop a square of carob into each piece of dough and form a round bread roll or any chosen shape around the carob, or you make a Carob Spread and put a teaspoonful of this into each piece of dough for a softer, runnier carob filling.

Place on baking sheets, cover, and allow to double in size. Brush with milk or lightly beaten egg and bake for 15 minutes. Remove from oven and cool a little before eating. This bread is also nice the day after baking.

Pâtisserie

We have talked about wholemeal flour in the introduction to the recipes for cakes, but with gâteaux you will find greater use of the whisked sponge method. This is a fantastic way to introduce air into cakes and gâteaux made with wholemeal flour. It has the advantage of not adding more sodium to the cakes which baking powder will do, although you can always choose to use salt-free baking powder.

Instead of double cream and a large number of egg yolks, strained yoghurts and low-fat cheeses give the creamy texture and bulk to the mixtures. Lightness is introduced by whisking egg yolks with honey and by using whisked egg whites. Honey is used in preference to sugar in some recipes because less is needed, although it *is* still a sugar. Desserts based on choux pastry use 81% wholemeal flour rather than 100%, because the results with 100% can be rather disappointing. This is really the only exception to the 100% rule.

Desserts & Gâteaux

Tia Mousse

SERVES 4–6

This is a very dark and rich mousse for special occasions.
It is quite close in texture compared with other mousses
and soufflés, and is best served in individual serving
glasses or dishes.

½ oz/12 g gelatine
boiling water
1 tablespoon decaffeinated coffee granules
1 tablespoon carob powder
2 free-range eggs, separated
2 oz/50 g fructose
8 oz/225 g low-fat curd *or* cream cheese
1 tablespoon Tia Maria coffee liqueur

decoration

coffee grounds (filter fine) and Greek yoghurt *or*
Chantilly Piping Cream (p. 22–3)

Sprinkle the gelatine onto 4 tablespoons of boiling water and stir to
dissolve. Dissolve the coffee granules in 1 tablespoon of boiling water and
add the carob powder to make a paste. Whisk together the egg yolks and
fructose until pale and creamy. Blend the carob mixture into the egg yolks,
followed by the cheese and Tia Maria. Whisk the egg whites until they form
stiff peaks.

Mix the cooled gelatine thoroughly into the mousse mixture and fold in
the egg whites when the mousse is on the point of setting. Carefully spoon
into the serving dishes and place in the fridge to set and chill. Decorate with
coffee grounds very finely sprinkled on a thin layer of Greek yoghurt, or
with piped Chantilly Cream.

Desserts & Gâteaux

Hazelnut Gâteau

SERVES 8–10

3 free-range eggs
3 tablespoons clear honey
4 oz/100 g ground hazelnuts
2 oz/50 g wholemeal flour, sieved

carob frosting

1 × 60 g bar plain carob, broken into pieces
1 oz/25 g soft margarine
4 tablespoons skimmed milk
¼ oz/6 g gelatine
4 tablespoons boiling water
8 oz/225 g strained Greek yoghurt
4 oz/100 g hazelnuts

filling

4 tablespoons no-added-sugar jam

Lightly oil an 8-in (20-cm) cake tin, and set the oven to 350°F/180°C/Gas 4.

Place the eggs and honey in an electric mixer and whisk until thick and ropy in consistency – until you can write your initials by drizzling the mixture from the whisk. (If you do not have an electric mixer whisk the mixture in a basin over a pan of hot water to speed up the process.) Fold in the ground hazelnuts using a metal tablespoon, and then fold in the sieved flour. Pour into the prepared tin and bake for 25 minutes. Remove from the heat and cool.

When cold slice horizontally into 3 layers. The sponge is quite crumbly, so this needs to be done carefully. If you are not confident, slice it in half only.

To make the frosting, place the carob pieces in a double boiler or in a basin standing in a pan of hot water, and add the margarine and milk. Melt together over a low heat, then remove and leave on one side. Sprinkle the gelatine onto the hot water and stir to dissolve. Stir the gelatine into the carob mixture and then allow to cool a little before carefully adding the yoghurt, a little at a time. Cool and refrigerate. Toast the hazelnuts, then finely dice, reserving 8–10 whole for decorating the top.

To assemble the gâteau, spread a layer of jam over the base and middle sections, and reassemble the cake. Spread the set frosting over the top and sides of the gâteau using a palette knife (most easily accomplished if you have an icing turntable). Press the diced nuts into the sides of the gâteau and arrange the 8 or 10 whole nuts around the top circumference, the number of nuts depending on the number of portions you intend to cut.

Desserts & Gâteaux

Carob Slices

MAKES 6

2 oz/50 g soft margarine
3 oz/75 g wholemeal flour
1 oz/25 g cornflour
3 free-range eggs
3 oz/75 g clear honey
1 quantity Carob Frosting (p. 77)
½ × 60 g plain carob, grated

Line a 7-in (17.5-cm) square baking tin with greaseproof paper, and set the oven to 350°F/180°C/Gas 4.

Melt the margarine over a low heat and remove to cool. Sieve together the flour and cornflour. Whisk the eggs and honey in an electric mixer until thick and ropy in consistency. (If you do not have an electric mixer use a hand whisk, placing the ingredients in a bowl over a pan of hot water to speed up the process.) Carefully fold the melted margarine and flour into the egg mixture, and pour into the prepared tin. Bake on the top shelf for 30 minutes. When cooked remove from the oven and allow to cool on a wire cooling tray.

Peel off the paper and slice into 6 portions. If you are able, slice each into 3 horizontally, but if you find this difficult slice them into 2. Reassemble with carob frosting between each layer then spread the sides and top of the slices with carob frosting. Press the grated carob onto the sides of the slices.
Refrigerate before serving.

Desserts & Gâteaux

Peach and Carob Cheesecake

SERVES 6

6 oz/175 g wholemeal digestive biscuits
1½ × 60 g bars no added sugar plain carob
4 tablespoons skimmed milk
3 ripe peaches
8 oz/225 g low-fat curd cheese
4 tablespoons orange juice
½ oz/12 g gelatine

Lightly oil an 8-in (20-cm) springform or loose-bottomed cake tin or flan ring.

Crush the biscuits to crumbs by placing in a polythene bag and pounding with a rolling pin. Place one carob bar, broken into pieces, and all the milk in the top of a double boiler or in a basin standing in a pan of hot water, and melt. Pour into the mixing bowl with the biscuit crumbs and stir well, then press into the base of the prepared tin and chill in the refrigerator.

Skin the peaches. (If they are not ripe and will not skin easily, then pour boiling water over them and leave to stand for 2 minutes before plunging into cold water. The skins should then come off easily.) Roughly chop and place in a liquidiser or food processor and blend to a purée. Put the cheese in a mixing bowl and stir in the purée. Place the orange juice in a saucepan and sprinkle on the gelatine. Place over a low heat and stir until dissolved. Cool a little and when on point of setting stir into the cheese mixture. Do make sure you stir the gelatine in thoroughly. Grate in the remaining half carob bar and stir well.

Pour onto the prepared base and return to the refrigerator to set and chill.

Decorate, if liked, with slices of peach and more grated carob.

Desserts & Gâteaux

Poires Belle Hélène

SERVES 4

This is a delicious mixture of cold ice-cream, warm poached pears and a hot carob sauce. Use Vanilla Carob Chip Ice-cream (p. 101), or make the ice cream without the carob chip as plain vanilla for this recipe. Alternatively you could buy a good quality vanilla ice-cream and just make the Carob Sauce yourself.

2 ripe but firm pears
1 cinnamon stick
1 quantity Vanilla Carob Chip Ice-cream (p. 101)

carob sauce

1 × 60 g bar no-added-sugar plain carob, broken into pieces
½ pint/300 ml half cream *or* ¼ pint/150 ml single cream
and ¼ pint/150 ml skimmed milk

Peel the pears and halve and core them. Place in a saucepan with enough water to almost cover, add the cinnamon stick, and cover with a lid. Poach over a low heat for about 15 minutes until cooked, but not mushy. Carefully remove from the saucepan and place in the individual serving dishes.

To make the sauce, melt the carob in the top of a double boiler or in a basin standing in a pan of hot water. Stir in the half cream or the cream and milk, and mix well for a few minutes until the carob has completely combined.

Place a couple of scoops of ice-cream in each dish alongside each pear half, and pour the hot sauce over them.

Desserts & Gâteaux

Class Coeurs à la Crème are deliciously different made with
carob mint chips on a coulis of kiwi fruit and mango,
page 92, and Carob Pears, poached pears coated with a
carob mousse, page 86, are very grown-up

Ánything is possible with carob, even sophisticated Carob Soufflé, page 83, and
Petits Pots au Carob, page 93

Carob Banana Mousse

SERVES 6

This is especially popular with children (and parents, too, have been known to have second helpings!).

½ oz/12 g gelatine
6 tablespoons boiling water
3 free-range eggs, separated
2 oz/50 g light muscovado sugar
1 × 60 g bar plain carob, broken into pieces
2 ripe bananas, about 3 oz/75 g each
juice of ½ lemon
8 oz/225 g strained Greek yoghurt

garnish
banana slices brushed with lemon juice
grated carob

Sprinkle the gelatine onto the boiling water and stir to dissolve. Whisk the egg yolks and sugar together until pale, creamy and thick. Melt the carob bar in the top of a double boiler or in a basin standing in a pan of hot water. Gradually blend the carob into the egg-yolk mixture. Mash the bananas roughly and blend in a liquidiser with the lemon juice and yoghurt, then fold into the mixture. Whisk the egg whites until they form stiff peaks and fold into the mousse.

Pour into a size 2 soufflé dish or into individual serving dishes or glasses. Garnish with thin slices of banana (brushed with lemon juice to prevent browning) and some grated carob.

Desserts & Gâteaux

Hot Carob Soufflé

SERVES 4

1 oz/25 g margarine
1 oz/25 g wholemeal flour
½ pint/300 ml skimmed milk
2 free-range eggs, separated
2 drops of natural vanilla essence
1 × 60 g bar plain carob, broken into pieces
1 tablespoon rum (optional)

Lightly oil and flour a size 2 soufflé dish, and heat the oven to 350°F/180°C/Gas 4.

Place the margarine and flour in a saucepan and stir over the heat to make a roux (thick paste). Gradually add the milk, stirring all the time to prevent lumps forming. Take off the heat and beat in the egg yolks and the vanilla essence. Melt the carob bar in a double boiler or a basin standing in a pan of hot water. Stir the melted carob and rum into the white sauce, mixing well. Whisk the egg whites until they form stiff peaks and fold into the sauce.

Pour at once into the prepared soufflé dish and bake for 40 minutes. Serve at once, dusting the top with a little carob powder, if liked.

Mocha Pots

MAKES 4

These little cold custards have a delightful coffee flavour with a slightly gooey carob layer on the base.

2 tablespoons demerara sugar
1 tablespoon skimmed milk powder
½ pint/300 ml hot decaffeinated coffee
2 free-range eggs
½ oz/12 g toasted hazelnuts, finely chopped
1 × 60 g bar no-added-sugar plain carob, grated

Set the oven to 350°F/180°C/Gas 4. Place 4 ramekins in a roasting tin and fill the tin with hot water to come two-thirds up the sides of the ramekins (thus creating a bain marie).

Dissolve the sugar and milk powder in the coffee and leave to cool. Whisk the eggs until frothy, then add the coffee mixture. Stir in the hazelnuts and grated carob.

Pour the mixture into the ramekins. Bake for 35 minutes. Allow to cool and chill before serving.

Desserts & Gâteaux

Cold Carob Soufflé

SERVES 6

½ oz/12 g gelatine
4 tablespoons boiling decaffeinated coffee
3 free-range eggs, separated
2 oz/50 g fructose
1 × 60 g bar plain carob, broken into pieces
1 tablespoon rum (optional)
8 oz/225 g strained Greek yoghurt

garnish
extra grated carob bar
soft fruit
strained Greek yoghurt (optional)

Lightly oil a size 1 soufflé dish, and make a paper collar by tying bands of greaseproof paper around the sides of the dish to extend about 3 in (7.5 cm) higher than the top. Alternatively prepare 4 large ramekins in the same way.

Sprinkle the gelatine onto the boiling coffee and stir to dissolve. Leave on one side to cool. Whisk together the egg yolks and the fructose until thick, ropy and pale in colour. Melt the carob in a double boiler or in a basin standing in a pan of hot water. Blend into the whisked eggs and add the rum, if using. Blend in the yoghurt and when the gelatine mixture has cooled, mix it in thoroughly. Whisk the egg whites until they form stiff peaks and when the carob mixture is on the point of setting fold in the whites.

Turn at once into the prepared dish(es) and place in the fridge for a couple of hours before serving to set and chill. Before serving remove the paper collar and press grated carob around the edge of the soufflé. Decorate the top with strawberries or raspberries or other seasonal fruit, placing the fruit on little blobs of strained yoghurt, if liked.

Desserts & Gâteaux

Chestnut Roll

SERVES 10

This is a very gooey and rich dessert – for those who like
such confections – so take a close look at the ingredients
before you embark! It's nice served with plain biscuits
such as langues-de-chat.

1 lb/450 g can unsweetened chestnut purée
2 fl. oz/60 ml milk
2 oz/50 g strained Greek yoghurt
2 × 60 g bars plain carob, broken into pieces
8 oz/225 g medium- or low-fat curd cheese

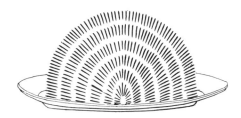

Place a sheet of greaseproof paper on a flat work-surface and have ready a
plastic kitchen ruler, if you have one.

Place the chestnut purée in a mixing bowl and beat with the milk, then
beat in the yoghurt. Spread onto the paper in an oblong about 10 × 6 in (25 ×
15 cm), using the ruler as guidance and to give straight edges. Melt the carob
bars in the top of a double boiler or in a basin standing in a pan of hot water.
Place the cheese in a mixing bowl and beat a little to soften. Pour in the
melted carob and beat well. Working quickly, because the carob mixture
stiffens, spread on top of the chestnut mixture in an even layer and then roll
up like a Swiss roll using the greaseproof paper to push the roll along. Keep
the roll firmly wrapped and place in the fridge at once to firm and chill for
about an hour.

Desserts & Gâteaux

Pineapple Pie

SERVES 8

In this recipe a crunchy biscuit base is topped with a parfait made from fresh pineapple. The whole 'cake' is frozen and served like an ice-cream cake. For those who feel in the mood for a slightly more fiddly exercise, it is attractive to pipe the words 'Pineapple Pie' on the top of the finished dessert before freezing.

7 oz/200 g digestive biscuits
3 oz/75 g soft margarine
1 tablespoon clear honey
½ × 60 g bar no-added-sugar plain carob, broken into pieces
grated nutmeg
1 large ripe pineapple
8 oz/225 g low-fat curd cheese
1 oz/25 g fructose
2 free-range egg whites

topping (optional)
½ × 60 g bar no-added-sugar plain carob, broken into pieces
½ oz/12 g soft margarine
½ tablespoon clear honey

Lightly oil a 7-in (17.5-cm) cake tin with a loose bottom.

Place the biscuits in a polythene bag and pound with a pestle or rolling pin to crush them to crumbs. Place the margarine, honey, carob and some nutmeg in a saucepan over a moderate heat and melt. Remove from heat and stir in the crumbs. Press into the base of the prepared tin and leave to set and chill in the freezer.

Cut away the outer skin of the pineapple and the central core if it is very hard and woody. Roughly chop the flesh into a liquidiser and blend to a purée. Place in a bowl and beat in the cheese and fructose. Whisk the egg whites until they form stiff peaks and fold into the pineapple mixture. Pour on top of the prepared base and return to the freezer.

For the topping, place the carob, margarine and honey in a saucepan and melt. Remove from heat and allow to thicken and cool before placing in a piping bag fitted with a writing nozzle and pipe the words 'Pineapple Pie' on the dessert. Return to the freezer until ready for use (usually after about 4 hours). Cut slices as needed.

NB If you don't have a piping bag with a writing nozzle you can make a bag and nozzle by rolling a piece of greaseproof paper into a cone with a thin hole at the end – but it can be a bit messy!

Desserts & Gâteaux

Carob Pears

MAKES 6

This dessert looks very impressive. The pears, coated in a layer of carob 'mousse' stand upright on a lake of more dark carob mousse.

1 × 60 g bar plain carob, broken into pieces
2 tablespoons decaffeinated black coffee
1 oz/25 g soft margarine
2 free-range eggs, separated
6 pears
2 oz/50 g toasted hazelnuts, chopped
2 strips of angelica

Melt the carob and coffee together in the top of a double boiler or in a basin standing in a pan of hot water. Remove from the heat and stir in the margarine. When the mixture has cooled, beat in the egg yolks. Whisk the egg whites until stiff and fold 2 tablespoons into the carob mixture to lighten it. Fold in the remainder of the egg whites. Peel the pears, leaving the stalks in place. Core them from the base and fill with the chopped nuts. Place the pears on a serving dish and spoon over the carob mousse until they are completely covered. The surplus will make a carob 'lake' around the base of the pears.

To make angelica pear leaves, soak the angelica in hot water for a few minutes to soften, then flatten with a palette knife and cut into triangular leaves using a sharp knife. Pierce the pears on each side just below the stalk and slip the leaves into the slits.

Desserts & Gâteaux

Strawberry Choux Ring

SERVES 6

¼ pint/150 ml water
2 oz/50 g unsalted butter
2½ oz/65 g 81% wholemeal flour
½ oz/12 g carob powder
2 free-range eggs

filling

1 teaspoon gelatine
4 tablespoons boiling water
1 oz/25 g skimmed milk powder
8 fl. oz/250 ml cold water
1 × 60 g bar no-added-sugar plain carob, broken into pieces
2 drops natural vanilla essence
8 oz/225 g strawberries

Lightly oil a baking sheet and set the oven to 400°F/200°C/Gas 6. Fit a piping bag with a plain 1-in (2.5-cm) nozzle.

Place the water and butter in a saucepan and bring to the boil. Remove from the heat and stir until the butter has melted. Sieve the flour and carob powder into the water and beat vigorously with a wooden spoon until the mixture forms a thick paste and leaves the sides of the pan cleanly in a shiny ball. Leave to cool for 3 minutes. Lightly beat the eggs and gradually beat a little at a time into the paste, beating well between additions. Do not allow the paste to become too soft: it must hold its shape when piped, so omit a little egg, if necessary. Place the paste in the piping bag and pipe into a circle about 7–8 in (17.5–20 cm) in diameter, building the circle as deeply as possible. Bake for 15 minutes then reduce the heat to 350°F/180°C/Gas 4 for a further 10 minutes. Remove from the oven and cool on a wire tray.

To make the carob filling sprinkle the gelatine onto the hot water and stir until dissolved. Sprinkle the skimmed milk powder onto the 8 fl. oz (250 ml) cold water and place in a saucepan over a moderate heat. Melt the carob bar in the top of a double boiler or in a basin standing in a pan of hot water. While it is melting gradually pour a little of the hot milk onto the carob, stirring all the time, until the mixture can be easily poured into the milk pan. Add the vanilla essence and continue stirring until the milk and carob are well mixed. Remove from the heat and stir in the gelatine. Pour through a sieve into a basin and allow to cool and set. Refrigerate. The mixture will set like a blancmange in the fridge so it needs whisking before use – thin, if liked, with a little natural yoghurt or milk, when whisking.

When the choux ring is cold, slice it in half horizontally and fill it with the carob filling and sliced or chopped fresh strawberries.

Desserts & Gâteaux

Carob Peach Roulade

SERVES 8

A deliciously light carob Swiss roll filled with a low-calorie peachy mousse, best served chilled and decorated with slices of fresh peach.

3 free-range eggs
3 tablespoons clear honey
3 oz/75 g wholemeal flour
1 oz/25 g carob powder
1 tablespoon boiling water

filling
2 ripe peaches
4 oz/100 g strained Greek yoghurt
½ oz/12 g gelatine
4 tablespoons orange juice

Lightly oil and line a Swiss roll tin with greaseproof paper, and set the oven to 400°F/200°C/Gas 6.

Whisk the eggs and honey together until thick and ropy. Sieve together the flour and carob powder and, using a metal tablespoon, fold into the egg mixture with the boiling water. Pour into the prepared tin and bake for 15 minutes, until firm and springy to the touch. Remove from the oven and invert onto a clean piece of greaseproof paper. Peel off the paper in which the roll was cooked, trim the edges and roll up. Leave on a wire cooling rack.

While the sponge is cooking, prepare the filling. Pour boiling water onto the peaches and then plunge into cold water. Peel off the skins, then roughly chop the flesh and place in a liquidiser with the yoghurt and blend to a purée. Sprinkle the gelatine over the orange juice in a small basin over a saucepan of hot water and stir to dissolve, then cool. When the gelatine is on the point of setting stir into the peach purée. Carefully unroll the cooled roulade and spread with the peach mixture. Re-roll and chill until served.

Desserts & Gâteaux

Orpheus would have been quite happy down under with a Carob Ice-
Cream like this one, page 29

Carob Fudge Cake with a thick Carob Frosting, pages 26–7, is decorated on top with grated carob for good measure

Start the day the French way with a carob-filled wholemeal or
granary croissant, page 73

Make it a Carob Birthday Cake this year, page 108, and add some
Carob-coated Crunch Bars, page 104, and Carob Popcorn, page 106, to take
home instead of sugary sweets

Carob Crêpes

MAKES 14

If you have no fresh skimmed milk, crêpes can be made with 2 tablespoons of dried skimmed milk powder whisked into ½ pint/300 ml cold water. This produces a slightly lighter crêpe. Make the filling first so that it can be chilled thoroughly before serving with the hot crêpes.

3 oz/75 g wholemeal flour
1 oz/25 g carob powder
1 free-range egg, lightly beaten
½ pint/300 ml skimmed milk
soy or corn oil

coffee and chestnut filling
1 tablespoon decaffeinated coffee granules
1 tablespoon boiling water
4 oz/100 g unsweetened chestnut purée
4 oz/100 g strained Greek yoghurt
1 tablespoon fructose

Sieve together the flour and carob powder and place in a bowl. Make a well in the centre and pour in the lightly beaten egg. Using a fork, gradually begin to beat the flour into the egg, working slowly from the well towards the edge of the bowl, adding milk as necessary to thin the mixture. Give a final whisk when all the milk is combined.

To make the crêpes, place a heavy-based omelette pan over a high heat and add a few drops of soy or corn oil. When the oil is hot (but not smoking), add about 2 tablespoons of batter, tipping the pan from side to side to ensure a thin, even layer. Cook until the batter has set then slip a palette knife under the crêpe and flip it over to cook for a minute on the other side. (When making a batch of crêpes I find it easy to pour the batter into the pan using a small cream jug which sits in a saucer on the side, to prevent any sticky drips or mess.)

To make the filling, dissolve the coffee granules in the water, then cool. Place the chestnut purée in a food processor or liquidiser and add the cooled coffee, yoghurt and fructose. Blend to a smooth purée, and chill.

Spread some chilled filling onto each hot crêpe, roll up and serve.

Desserts & Gâteaux

Carob Mousse Gâteau

SERVES 6

This dessert is based on Michel Roux's 'Rozenn aux Parfums d'Orange Mentholés' which he has demonstrated to audiences of cookery enthusiasts during one of his too few public demonstrations, and which features on his restaurant menus.

3 oz/75 g ground almonds
grated rind and juice of ½ orange
3 free-range eggs
2 oz/50 g light muscovado sugar
3 oz/75 g wholemeal flour

mousse filling
2 × 60 g bars no-added-sugar plain carob, broken into pieces
¼ pint/150 ml decaffeinated black coffee
½ oz/12 g soft margarine
½ oz/12 g gelatine
4 tablespoons boiling water
3 free-range eggs, separated
2 oz/50 g fructose
a tiny pinch of ground cinnamon
¼ pint/150 ml natural yoghurt

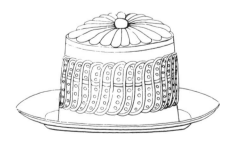

Desserts & Gâteaux

Lightly oil and line a 7-in (17.5-cm) cake ring, place on a baking sheet, and set the oven to 400°F/200°C/Gas 6.

Whisk together the ground almonds, orange rind and juice, 1 whole egg and 2 egg yolks, plus the sugar, until increased in volume, pale in colour and nearly thick (it will not thicken as much as a Swiss roll mixture). Sieve the flour and fold into the mixture. Whisk the egg whites until they form stiff peaks and fold in. Pour into the prepared ring and bake for 20 minutes. Remove and allow to cool on a wire tray. When cold cut into 4 layers: you will only need 2 for this dessert so the other 2 can be frozen, or stored in an airtight tin and used at a later date for a cake or gâteau.

To make the mousse, melt the carob bars in the top of a double boiler or in a basin standing in a pan of hot water. Make the coffee and add to the carob, stirring all the time. Add the margarine, melt, then remove from the heat. Sprinkle the gelatine onto the water and stir until dissolved (until the liquid is transparent). Leave to cool. Beat the egg yolks into the carob mixture, 1 at a time, and add the fructose and cinnamon. Stir in the yoghurt carefully, then add the gelatine. When on the point of setting, whisk the egg whites until they hold firm peaks and fold into the carob mixture.

To assemble, place 1 slice of the cut gâteau on a flat tray and place the cake ring around it. Fill with mousse until near the top of the ring. Place the second piece of gâteau on top. Leave in the fridge for an hour to firm and set, then remove the ring and mask the top and sides of the gâteau with the rest of the mousse. Refrigerate until ready to serve

Mint Coeur á la Crème

MAKES 6

These delicious desserts are traditionally made with cream cheese and whipped double cream, but this version uses lower-fat and lower-calorie curd cheese plus strained yoghurt for the same creamy texture with the innovative flavour of carob mint chips.

8 oz/225 g low-fat curd cheese
8 oz/225 g strained Greek yoghurt
1 tablespoon fructose
½ × 60 g carob mint bar, finely chopped
3 free-range egg whites

Line 6 ceramic perforated coeur à la crème moulds with butter muslin and stand them in a tray such as a Swiss roll tin which will fit inside your fridge.

Beat together the curd cheese and yoghurt to make a soft paste. Stir in the fructose. Stir the finely chopped carob into the mixture. Whisk the egg whites until they hold stiff peaks, fold in 2 tablespoons of egg white to lighten the mixture, then fold in the remainder. Spoon into the prepared moulds and place in the fridge to drain and chill.

Serve with a fresh fruit purée such as that made by liquidising, then straining, 12 oz/325 g fresh or thawed raspberries. Garnish with fresh mint leaves.

NB A plain carob chip version can be made by substituting ½ × 60 g plain carob bar for the mint bar and by adding a few drops of natural vanilla essence. Serve with fresh fruit purée as well.

Desserts & Gâteaux

Petits Pots au Carob

MAKES 4

1½ × 60 g bars no-added-sugar plain carob, broken into pieces
⅛ pint/75 ml water
2 tablespoons clear honey
½ oz/12 g gelatine
4 tablespoons cold water
4 free-range eggs, separated
1 tablespoon brandy *or* rum (optional)

Place the carob, ⅛ pint (75 ml) water and the honey in the top of a double boiler or in a basin standing in a pan of hot water. Sprinkle the gelatine onto the 4 tablespoons cold water, and place in a pan of hot water. Stir to dissolve. Remove the carob from the heat and allow to cool and thicken before beating in the egg yolks. (To speed the process, place the mixture in the freezer for a few minutes.) When the gelatine has also cooled, stir thoroughly into the mixture. Whisk the egg whites until they form stiff peaks and then fold into the mixture with the brandy or rum, if using.

Pour into 4 ramekins and allow to set and chill. Decorate the top with piped Chantilly Piping Cream (p. 22–3), and a Carob Rose Leaf (p. 96), or a raspberry or strawberry.

Desserts & Gâteaux

Baked Carob Cheesecake

SERVES 8

This is a most attractive cheesecake with the carob pastry case contrasting in colour and texture with the orange filling.

3 oz/75 g wholemeal flour
1 oz/25 g carob powder
2 oz/50 g soft vegetable margarine
water

filling
7 oz/200 g low-fat curd cheese
4 oz/100 g natural yoghurt
2 tablespoons clear honey
2 free-range eggs, separated
zest and juice of 1 orange
2 drops of orange oil

Lightly oil an 8-in (20-cm) flan ring and a baking tray, and set the oven to 350°F/180°C/Gas 4.

To make the pastry base, sieve together the flour and carob powder and rub in the fat until the mixture resembles breadcrumbs. Add a little water to make a soft dough, then roll out on a floured surface. Line the flan ring.

For the filling, place the cheese, yoghurt, honey, egg yolks and orange zest and juice in a bowl; mix thoroughly. Whisk the egg whites until they form stiff peaks and fold into the mixture with the orange oil. Pour into the prepared pastry case and bake for 45 minutes until the filling is set and golden brown. Remove, and allow to cool before serving.

Desserts & Gâteaux

Orange Cheesecake

SERVES 8

6 oz/175 g digestive biscuits
2 oz/50 g soft margarine
1 × 60 g bar no-added-sugar plain carob, broken into pieces
freshly grated nutmeg
juice and zest of 1 orange
½ oz/12 g gelatine
6 oz/175 g low-fat curd cheese
4 oz/100 g strained Greek yoghurt
2 drops orange oil
2 free-range eggs, separated

Lightly oil an 8-in (20-cm) loose-bottomed cake tin.

Place the biscuits in a bag and beat with a rolling pin or pestle to crush to crumbs. Melt together the margarine and carob bar in a double boiler or in a basin standing in a pan of hot water. Remove from heat and mix with the crumbs and grated nutmeg, press into the prepared tin and place in the fridge to set.

Squeeze the juice from the orange into a measuring jug and make up to ⅛ pint (75 ml) with cold water. Place in a saucepan or in a basin standing in a pan of hot water and sprinkle on the gelatine. Stir until dissolved then allow to cool.

Beat together the cheese and yoghurt, add the orange zest and oil, and an egg yolk (reserve the other for another dish). Whisk both egg whites until they form stiff peaks. Stir the cooled gelatine into the cheese mixture and then fold in the egg whites. Pour on top of the prepared base and smooth the top. Chill until set. Decorate, if liked, with grated orange zest, grated carob and slices of orange.

Desserts & Gâteaux

Carob Caraque

Melt 1 × 60 g no-added-sugar plain carob bar in the usual way – in the top of a double boiler or in a basin standing in a pan of hot water – and pour or spread over a cold surface such as a marble slab using a palette knife. When completely set, push a thin-bladed sharp knife across the carob at a slight angle using a gentle sawing movement to scrape off layers of carob that will form thin curls making long scrolls.

Grated Carob

This makes an attractive garnish to many carob (and other) dishes and is made simply by grating the bar of carob against a household cheese grater.

Carob Curls

These can be made by literally peeling off shavings of carob from a bar by using a potato peeler. Cool hands are best for this job. Shave either directly over the area to receive the carob, or onto a cool surface and remove the carob from this to garnish your dishes.

Carob Shapes

Squares, diamonds, triangles and circles can all be cut out of carob using a sharp knife and a ruler. Simply melt the carob in the usual way (see above) and then spread a thin even layer on a cold surface or a piece of greaseproof paper. When it has just set, but is not too hard and brittle, cut out the required shapes (use a biscuit or petits-fours cutter for the circles).

Carob Leaves

If you have in the garden some small rose leaves with well defined veins, then you can wash and dry them well and spread them with melted carob by coating the underside of each leaf using a brush or knife. After the carob has set the leaf may be carefully peeled away to reveal an attractive carob leaf.

Desserts & Gâteaux

Double cream and egg yolks are the classic ingredients for ice-cream, but you won't find the cream or the quantity of egg yolks in these recipes because they are consciously trying to give flavour without the fat. Most are based on a simple custard made with skimmed milk and using low-fat soft cheeses or strained yoghurt to give a creamy texture without the calories.

Using the basic custard or a strained yoghurt as a base, you can also experiment with your own favourite fruits to make ice-creams. Chopped carob makes a delicious addition to most flavours and it can also coat the ices you make to provide your own 'choc ice' bars and scoops. Use carob in its powdered form to flavour and sweeten the basic custards.

For the most delicious creamily smooth and home-made ice-cream the mixture should be churned or beaten as it freezes to prevent ice crystals forming. There is a complete guide to making ice-cream either with a machine or by hand on the following pages.

Ice-Cream

Making Ice-Cream

There are several ways to make ice-cream using special machines, or there is the old-fashioned method of preparing the ice cream then partially freezing it, removing it from the freezer and breaking up the ice crystals by beating the mixture before re-freezing it. This beating and refreezing may, in some instances, be done twice.

Personally, I think the best results are achieved by the better ice-cream machines because they can churn the ice-cream continuously as it freezes. This avoids the formation of ice crystals that can spoil otherwise delicious home-made ice-cream. Machine-made ice-cream also has a much better texture and appearance.

Ice-cream machines can be classified as those which fit *inside* the freezer and those which operate *outside* the freezer. All have paddles which churn the mixture as it freezes. The machines that fit inside the freezer are mostly electrically operated which means making sure you have a spare electric socket within reach of the freezer. I think they are inconvenient because they encourage the freezer to form frost, as the door is partially open for some time, and they are thus not as economical as they might be. The battery-operated ones which fit inside the freezer are very cheap, but they can make only small amounts of ice-cream at once, and they can run for only a limited time making their operation a little fussy in some instances.

I have achieved the best results with the middle of the range (price wise) machines from Salton and ICTC Electrical whose Gelatiera and Piccolo machines respectively are well designed and, in the case of the Piccolo especially, beautifully easy to use and to clean. They also make ice-cream making a simple process.

With the Piccolo, the machine's mixing bowl is frozen in the freezer overnight before use, then the ice-cream mixture is simply poured into it and the ice-cream may be ready with as little as 9 minutes' churning. It is then transferred to a mould or container and frozen. The Gelatiera requires ice cubes to be made which form an ice jacket outside the central bowl containing the ice-cream and paddle, and the ice-cream takes longer to make; but the results are good and if you work quickly you can get two batches made with the one lot of ice cubes whereas the Piccolo will really only make one batch before the bowl needs re-freezing.

If you do not have a machine ice-cream can be made 'by hand'. Pour or spoon the mixture into a container and cover, then place in the freezer for about an hour until half frozen. Remove and, using a fork, break up the mixture and beat well. Re-cover and return to the freezer. Repeat after a further hour and then refreeze until firm, or until the ice cream is required.

Ice-Cream

Before serving, transfer the ice cream from the freezer to the fridge for between 30 minutes and an hour to soften slightly and allow the flavour to come through.

One further point. A microwave oven is especially useful for ice-cream because it can make the basic custard for many ice-creams in minutes, and cuts out the stirring over a double saucepan which may take some time and is a warm job in summer when most ice-cream is made. Follow your own microwave oven's instruction booklet for making custards, but most simply heat the milk on high power for 2 minutes after which the milk is whisked onto the eggs and sugar and returned to the oven for a further 2–3 minutes, being stirred or whisked once or twice during cooking. Simple, isn't it?

Raspberry 'Choc' Ice

SERVES 6

8 oz/225 g strained Greek yoghurt
½ pint/300 ml buttermilk
8 oz/225 g raspberries
1 tablespoon fructose
2 × 60 g bars no-added-sugar plain carob, broken into pieces

Place the yoghurt, buttermilk and washed raspberries in a liquidiser and blend to a purée (or push through a sieve to make a purée). Blend in the fructose and make the ice-cream in your usual way.

When frozen, scoop out balls and open freeze for a couple of hours. Melt the carob in the top of a double boiler or in a basin standing in a pan of hot water. Holding the ice-cream balls on a skewer, dip into the melted carob, or spread carob over the scoops. Re-freeze on a wire baking tray, then store in a sealed container.

Ice-Cream

Carob Bombe

SERVES 6–8

Before you start making the ice-cream place the bombe
mould in the freezer to chill. Make the carob ice-cream
first because this is the one that will go into the mould
first, and while it is setting make the strawberry.

carob ice-cream
½ pint/300 ml skimmed milk
2 free-range eggs
1 tablespoon fructose
1 × 60 g bar plain carob, broken into pieces
4 oz/100 g quark

strawberry ice-cream
½ pint/300 ml skimmed milk
1 tablespoon fructose
2 free-range eggs
8 oz/225 g strawberries
4 oz/100 g quark

For the carob ice-cream, place the milk in a saucepan or a double boiler and
heat until just below boiling point. Remove from the heat. Whisk the eggs
and fructose together and pour the milk onto them, whisking all the time.
Return to a clean pan through a sieve, and stir over the heat until the
custard thickens – do not allow the mixture to boil or it will curdle. When
thickened remove from the heat and allow to cool. Melt the carob bar by
placing in a double boiler or standing in a basin in a pan of hot water and
blend in with the quark then blend this mixture into the cooled custard and
make the ice-cream in your usual way. When it is beginning to freeze well
line the inside of the bombe mould with a thick layer, shaping it with the
back of a spoon. Return to the freezer for a couple of hours before filling the
centre of the bombe with strawberry ice-cream.

  To make the strawberry ice-cream, follow the same procedure as for the
carob ice-cream, but instead of blending the melted carob and quark
together blend the quark and strawberries in a liquidiser, or by pushing
through a sieve. The cooled custard is then mixed in and the ice-cream
made in your usual way.

NB The two recipes have been given separately so you may use them as
individual recipes, but you could always make double the quantity of
custard in one go and then halve it and blend each half into the carob and
strawberry mixtures.

Ice-Cream

Carob Chip Ice-Cream

SERVES 4

This is also nice made with mint-flavoured carob.

½ pint/300 ml skimmed milk
1 vanilla pod
2 free range eggs
1 tablespoon fructose
½ pint/300 ml half cream
1 × 60 g bar no-added-sugar plain carob, finely chopped

Place the milk in a pan and add the vanilla pod (cut into quarters to release more flavour) to the milk. Heat until almost boiling then remove and leave to infuse for 15 minutes. Whisk the eggs and fructose together then pour on the milk, whisking all the time. Strain the mixture back into a clean saucepan or double boiler, and stir over a moderate heat until the custard thickens. Remove from the heat and allow to cool before pouring in the half cream. Add the finely chopped carob bar, and stir in well before making the ice-cream in your usual way.

Carob Praline Ice-Cream

SERVES 4

½ pint/300 ml skimmed milk
1 tablespoon carob powder dissolved in 1 tablespoon water
2 free-range egg yolks
1½ oz/40 g demerara sugar
3 oz/75 g flaked almonds
8 oz/225 g strained Greek yoghurt

Place the milk in a saucepan or double boiler and heat until just below boiling point. Remove from the heat and mix with the carob paste. Lightly beat the egg yolks and pour the milk onto them, whisking all the time. Return to a clean pan through a sieve and stir over a moderate heat until the custard thickens – do not allow the mixture to boil or it will curdle.

When thickened remove from heat and allow to cool. Place the sugar and nuts in the bottom of a large, flat, heavy saucepan and stand over a low heat until the sugar has melted and the nuts are coated in it. Remove and spread on a flat tray until cold and crisp. Then place the praline in a food processor or coffee grinder and grind to a powder or chop very finely. Blend the cooled custard in with the yoghurt and fold in the praline. Make ice-cream in your usual way.

Ice-Cream

Blackcurrant and Carob Mint Chip

SERVES 4

½ pint/300 ml skimmed milk
1 tablespoon fructose
2 free-range egg yolks
8 oz/225 g blackcurrants
4 oz/100 g low-fat cream cheese
½ × 60 g bar mint carob, finely chopped

Place the milk in a saucepan or double boiler and heat until just below boiling point. Remove from heat. Whisk the fructose and egg yolks together and pour the milk onto them, whisking all the time. Return to a clean pan through a sieve and stir over the heat until the custard thickens – do not allow to boil or the mixture will curdle. When thickened remove from the heat to cool.

Wash the blackcurrants and place in a saucepan with a few tablespoons of cold water and cook until the juices begin to run. Remove from the heat and when cool liquidise with the cream cheese. Blend in the custard and finely chopped mint carob. Stir into the mixture and make ice-cream in your usual way.

Mocha Ice-Cream

SERVES 4

½ pint/300 ml skimmed milk
1 tablespoon fructose
2 free-range eggs
2½ fl. oz/75 ml black decaffeinated coffee
1 dessertspoon decaffeinated ground coffee (filter fine)
1 × 60 g bar no-added-sugar plain carob, broken into pieces
4 oz/100 g quark
2 oz/50 g curd cheese

Place the milk in a saucepan or double boiler and heat until just below boiling point. Remove from heat. Whisk the fructose and eggs together and pour the milk onto them, whisking all the time. Return to a clean pan through a sieve and stir over the heat until the custard thickens – do not allow the mixture to boil or it will curdle. When thickened remove from the heat and allow to cool.

Blend the cooled coffee into the custard with the coffee grounds. Melt the carob in the top of a double boiler or in a basin standing in a pan of hot water. Blend with the quark and curd cheese then blend this mixture into the custard and make the ice-cream in your usual way.

Ice-Cream

Chocolate is a favourite for many children. These recipes use carob to provide treats especially popular with children, but made more nutritious than the average shop-bought item because they are made from wholemeal flour, unsaturated fats, less sugar and other items such as oats and dried fruits and nuts.

Establishing cakes and sweets as a 'treat' rather than an everyday food is difficult, especially when many children spend their 'dinner money' in the sweetshop first thing in the morning. But perhaps putting a home-made goodie in the lunchbox may be one way to cut down on the consumption of highly refined sugary goods.

Home-made goodies are also free from the artificial colourings and other additives used to give foods which are designed to appeal to children their garish attraction. As an added bonus they are lower in fats and sugars and higher in fibre.

Children's Corner

Fudge Fingers

MAKES 12

Although this is one for the kids, it was very popular
with the grown ups when tested!

1½ × 60 g bars no-added-sugar plain carob, broken into pieces
2 oz/50 g soft margarine
2 tablespoons clear honey
6 oz/175 g digestive biscuits
1 oz/25 g desiccated coconut

Lightly oil a 7-in (17.5 cm) square baking tin. Or you can also use a round cake tin and cut the fudge into wedges.

Place the carob bars, margarine and honey in a saucepan over a low heat and melt. Place the biscuits in a polythene bag and crush by pounding with a pestle or a rolling pin to make crumbs. Remove the carob mixture from the heat and stir into the crumbs. Press into the base of the prepared tin, sprinkle the top with coconut and press in, then chill until set. Cut into fingers or wedges.

Carob-coated Crunch Bars

MAKES 16

4 oz/100 g soft margarine
3 oz/75 g demerara sugar
2 tablespoons clear honey
8 oz/225 g rolled oats
1½ × 60 g bars plain carob, broken into pieces

Lightly oil a rectangular Swiss roll tin, 6 × 10 in (15 × 25 cm) and set the oven to 350°F/180°C/Gas 4.

Place the margarine, sugar and honey in a saucepan and melt over a low heat. Remove from the heat and stir in the oats. Press into the prepared tin and bake for 25–30 minutes until golden brown. Remove from the oven and cut into fingers, but do not remove from the tin. When cold cut through again and remove the fingers from the tin.

Melt the carob over a gentle heat in the top of a double boiler, or in a basin standing in a pan of hot water. Using a palette knife cover first the sides of the bars and then the bases, leaving them face down on the cooling tray for the carob to set. Store in an airtight tin.

Children's Corner

* Fudge Fingers

Banana Muffins

* Spread more honey
on top before pressing
coconut on top

Raisin Bars

MAKES 14

3½ oz/90 g soft margarine
2 oz/50 g light muscovado sugar
1 free-range egg
3 drops of natural vanilla essence
3 oz/75 g medium oatmeal
3 oz/75 g wholemeal flour, sieved
4 oz/100 g large seedless raisins
1 × 60 g bar no-added-sugar plain carob, finely chopped
a little milk, if needed

Lightly oil a Swiss roll tin and set the oven to 350°F/180°C/Gas 4.

Beat together the margarine, sugar, egg and vanilla until light and fluffy. Stir in the oatmeal, flour and raisins. Stir in the finely chopped carob bar as well. Add a little milk to bind the mixture, if necessary. Turn into the prepared tin and bake for 25 minutes.

Remove from the oven and allow to cool a little before cutting into fingers. Remove from the tin when cold. Store in an airtight tin.

Banana Muffins

MAKES 6

These muffins are very filling and have a soft, moist texture. They make excellent portable breakfasts for late risers or tardy school pupils.

2 oz/50 g carrot, grated
2 oz/50 g banana, mashed
3 oz/75 g soft margarine
2 oz/50 g clear honey
1 oz/25 g oatmeal
4 oz/100 g muesli
1 × 60 g bar no-added-sugar plain carob, finely chopped

Lightly oil a muffin or cake pan with 6 deep cups, and set the oven to 325°F/160°C/Gas 3.

Cream the carrot and banana together with the margarine, honey and oatmeal. Fold in the muesli and the finely chopped carob bar, and spoon the mixture into the prepared baking pan. Bake for 30 minutes.

Allow to cool slightly before removing from the pan to finish cooling on a wire cooling rack.

Children's Corner

Carob Popcorn

Add about 1 oz (25 g) chopped nuts to the mixture too,
for a change. Much healthier than sweets.

2 oz/50 g popcorn
1 tablespoon corn or soy oil
½ × 60 g bar plain carob, broken into pieces
1 tablespoon clear honey
½ oz/12 g unsalted butter

Place the oil in the bottom of a heavy-based saucepan with a well fitting lid of at least 2.2 pints/1 litre and heat until hot, but not smoking. Drop in the popcorn and cover with the lid. Shake the pan every few moments and soon you will hear the corn beginning to pop. When the popping has stopped remove from the heat. It is necessary to keep shaking the pan to prevent the corn from burning or sticking.

Melt the carob in the top of a double boiler or place in a basin standing in a pan of hot water. Remove from the heat and add the honey and butter. Pour onto the popcorn in a large mixing bowl and toss well to cover the popcorn.
Delicious hot and cold.

Carob Junket

SERVES 4

1 pint/600 ml milk
1 oz/25 g clear honey (optional)
1 × 60 g bar no-added-sugar plain carob, broken into pieces
1 dessertspoon rennet

Heat the milk in a saucepan with the honey and carob, stirring to dissolve the carob. Pour into a bowl and allow to cool to 98°F/36°C. Stir in the rennet and pour into individual serving dishes. (You cannot use a mould with rennet as you can with blancmange, because rennet does not give a firm enough set to allow the junket to be turned out.) Decorate with a little extra grated carob and orange or lemon zest.

NB   Carob powder mixed with cold milk or water to make a paste can be used instead of carob bars.

Children's Corner

Carob Blancmange

SERVES 4

1 pint/600 ml milk
1 tablespoon carob powder
1½–2 tablespoons potato flour
½ tablespoon light muscovado sugar

Place the milk in a saucepan, reserving 2 fl. oz (60 ml), and heat until almost boiling. Blend the carob powder, potato flour and sugar together in the reserved milk to make a paste. Pour the hot milk onto the paste, stirring all the time. Return to a clean pan and stir until thickened. (Sometimes the mixture will thicken enough when the milk is poured on without returning to the pan.)

Pour into a wetted mould – a rabbit one would be good – and leave to set. Chill before turning out of the mould and serving.

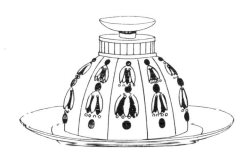

Muesli Munchies

MAKES 12

4 oz/100 g soft margarine
4 tablespoons clear honey
1 × 60 g bar no-added-sugar plain carob, broken into pieces
8 oz/225 g muesli

Melt the margarine, honey and carob together in a saucepan over a moderate heat, stirring to combine the ingredients. Remove from the heat and stir in the muesli.

Drop a dessertspoonful into each of 12 paper cake cases and leave in the refrigerator to firm up. They are nice served chilled.

Children's Corner

Carob Birthday Cake

SERVES 10

1 × 60 g bar no-added-sugar plain carob, broken into pieces
4 tablespoons water
1 tablespoon carob powder
4 oz/100 g soft margarine
4 oz/100 g clear honey
3 free-range eggs
8 oz/225 g wholemeal flour
1 teaspoon salt-free baking powder

filling

no-added-sugar raspberry jam

frosting

1 × 60 g bar no-added-sugar plain carob, broken into pieces
8 oz/225 g strained Greek yoghurt

Lightly oil a 7- or 8-in (17.5- or 20-cm) cake tin, and set the oven to 350°F/180°C/Gas 4.

Melt the carob bar with the water in the top of a double boiler or in a basin standing in a pan of hot water. Remove from heat and stir in the carob powder. Cream together the margarine and honey until pale and light, and gradually beat in the eggs, beating well between additions. Blend in the carob paste. Sieve the flour and baking powder together, and fold into the mixture. Spoon into the prepared tin, smoothing the top, and bake for 35 minutes.

Remove from oven and cool on a wire tray. When cold cut in half and sandwich together with jam. To make the frosting, melt the carob in the top of a double boiler or in a basin standing in a pan of hot water. Gradually blend into the yoghurt and spread over the cake as a frosting. A birthday message can be written on the top using extra melted carob or Carob Ganache (p. 25).

Children's Corner

Carob Flapjacks

MAKES 12

4 oz/100 g soft margarine
3 oz/75 g demerara sugar
2 tablespoons clear honey
1 tablespoon carob powder dissolved in 2 tablespoons water
8 oz/225 g rolled oats

Lightly oil a 7½-in (19-cm) square Swiss roll tin, and set the oven to 350°F/180°C/Gas 4.

Place the margarine, sugar and honey in a saucepan and melt. Remove from the heat and stir in the carob. When mixed well, stir in the oats and press lightly into the prepared tin. Bake for 25–30 minutes.

Remove from the oven and cut into fingers, but do not remove from the tin. When cold cut through again and remove the fingers, leaving them to become completely cold before storing in an airtight tin.

Children's Corner

If you have ever read the ingredients' panel on hot chocolate drinks, chocolate milk shakes, cocoa powders and other bedtime drinks you will have noticed that they contain sugar, salt, artificial sweeteners and artificial additives in some form or another.

Using carob as a basis for home-made versions, you can avoid these ingredients – items which you might prefer not to have in your bedtime drink. You can regulate the amount of added sugar and you will find that carob is sweeter than cocoa anyway.

Enjoy the flavour of carob sprinkled onto a cup of cappuccino, instead of cocoa, or try a sprinkling of ground cinnamon on top of your cup of hot carob.

Drinks

Carob Bar Shake

SERVES 1–2

⅓ × 60 g bar no-added-sugar plain carob, broken into pieces
4 tablespoons boiling water
½ pint/300 ml milk *or* soya milk

Melt the carob, with the water, in a double boiler or basin standing in a pan of hot water. Add to the milk in a liquidiser or blender and whisk well. Chill and then whisk again to give a frothy appearance and texture before serving. Top with a sprinkle of extra carob powder or ground cinnamon.

Hot Drinking Carob

SERVES 1–2

With this drink a sprinkling of cinnamon on top is nice.
You could also try a sprinkling of carob powder on top of
your cappuccino instead of cocoa.

½ pint/300 ml milk
1 piece of cinnamon bark
2 teaspoons carob powder
1 tablespoon water
1 teaspoon demerara sugar (optional)
ground cinnamon

Heat the milk with the cinnamon bark until just below boiling point. Blend the carob powder and water to a paste and pour on the milk. Stir well and add the sugar, if using (it is really quite sweet enough already!) Return to the pan to reheat, if necessary, then pour into a serving cup. Top with a sprinkle of ground cinnamon.

Carob Milk Shake

SERVES 1–2

1 level tablespoon carob powder
1 tablespoon boiling water
1 teaspoon honey (optional)
½ pint/300 ml milk *or* soya milk

Blend the carob powder and boiling water to a paste with the honey. Place the milk in a blender or liquidiser and add the carob. Whisk well. Chill before serving and whisk again to give the shake a frothy appearance and texture. Top with an extra sprinkling of carob powder.

Drinks

Minty Shake

SERVES 1–2

½ × 60 g bar mint carob, broken into pieces
2 tablespoons boiling water
½ pint/300 ml milk *or* soya milk

Place the mint carob bar and water in a saucepan and dissolve. Add to the milk and place both in a blender or liquidiser and whisk. Chill and then whisk again before serving.

As a special treat, add a scoop of carob ice-cream (p. 29) to the drink just after it has been poured.

Drinks

KEY TO FOLLOWING TABLES

CALS. = Calories
CARB. = Carbohydrate
PROT. = Protein
SOD. = Sodium
POT. = Potassium
CAFF. = Caffeine
THEOB. = Theobromine

Appendices

	CALORIES	SUGARS	FAT	FIBRE	CARBOHYDRATE	PROTEIN	SALT (mg)	CAFFEINE	THEOBROMINE
Cocoa powder	312	52	5·1	—	79	18·5	950	0·38	2·22
Carob powder	177	46	0·7	7	87·4	4·5	100	—	—
Drinking chocolate	366	73·8	6	—	77·4	5·5	250	0·1	0·55
Chocolate, plain	525	59·5	29·2	—	64·8	4·7	11	0·06	0·35
Chocolate, milk	529	56·5	30·3	—	59·4	8·4	120	0·01	0·07
Carob, plain	311	—	19·8	0·3	32·2	3·1	73	—	—
Carob, plain (no-added-sugar)	296	—	19·4	0·4	25·2	6·8	195	—	—

NUTRITIONAL CONTENT (GRAMS PER 100 GRAMS)

	SATURATED	MONOUNSATURATED	POLYUNSATURATED
Cocoa powder	60·5	34.8	3·0
Carob powder	less than 1·0 altogether		
Drinking chocolate	61·4	34·7	3·2
Chocolate, plain	62·3	33·6	3·2
Chocolate, milk	60·5	33·7	3·7
Carob, plain	10·2	17·8	5
Carob, plain (no-added-sugar)	10·1	17·9	5

FAT CONTENT (GRAMS PER 100 GRAMS)

Carob Black Forest Gâteau

	CALS. (g)	CARB. (g)	FAT (g)	PROT. (g)	FIBRE (g)	SOD. (mg)	POT. (mg)	IRON (mg)	CAFF. (mg)	THEOB. (mg)
4 free-range eggs	394	—	29.2	33	—	374	374	5.4	—	—
4oz/100g honey	288	76.4	—	0.4	—	11	51	0.4	—	—
5oz/150g wholemeal flour	397	82.25	2.5	16.5	12	3.75	450	5	—	—
1 tsp baking powder	5.82	1.35	—	0.18	—	421.5	1.75	—	—	—
1oz/25g carob powder	50.57	13.14	0.7	1.2	2	28.57	271.42	14.78	—	—
1 × 60g bar no-added-sugar plain carob	296	25.2	19.4	6.8	0.4	117	328.8	4.8	—	—
2 tsbs decaffeinated black coffee	—	—	—	—	—	—	—	—	—	—
8oz/225g strained Greek yoghurt	290	8.6	18	16.4	—	94	268	—	—	—
no added sugar black sugar jam	123	35	0	0.35	1.0	14	78	1	—	—
1 quantity Chantilly piping cream	346	8.6	18	30.2	—	232	543	0.24	—	—
60g plain carob	311	32.2	19.8	3.1	0.3	43.8	199.8	3.6	—	—
Total	**2501.39**	**282.74**	**107.6**	**108.13**	**15.7**	**1339.62**	**2565.77**	**34.82**	—	—

Chocolate Black Forest Gâteau

	CALS. (g)	CARB. (g)	FAT (g)	PROT. (g)	FIBRE (g)	SOD. (mg)	POT. (mg)	IRON (mg)	CAFF. (mg)	THEOB. (mg)
5 eggs	492.5	—	36.5	41.25	—	467.5	467.5	1.35	—	—
8oz/225g caster sugar	788	200	—	—	—	—	4	—	—	—
4oz/100g white flour	350	80	1.2	9.8	3.4	2	140	2.4	—	—
1 tbsp cornflour	44.25	11.5	0.08	0.075	—	6.5	1.62	0.17	—	—
1 tsp baking powder	5.82	1.35	—	0.18	—	421.5	1.75	—	—	—
1oz/25g cocoa powder	89.14	3.28	6.2	5.28	—	271.4	428.57	3	0.095	0.555
Filling										
½pint/300ml double cream	1028	4.6	110.86	3.45	—	62.1	181.7	0.46	—	—
1lb/450g can Morello cherries	349	88.3	0.9	3.9	1.2	4	543	1.3	—	—
2 tbsps Kirsch	63	—	—	—	—	—	—	—	—	—
2oz/50g caster sugar	197	100	—	—	—	—	1	—	—	—
Topping										
¼pint/150ml double cream	514.05	2.3	55.43	1.725	—	31.05	90.85	0.23	—	—
2oz/50g plain chocolate	265	32	15	2.35	—	11	300	2.4	0.08	0.5
Total	**4185.76**	**523.33**	**226.17**	**68.01**	**4.6**	**1277.05**	**2159.99**	**11.31**	**0.179**	**1.055**

Carob Profiteroles

	CALS. (g)	CARB. (g)	FAT (g)	PROT. (g)	FIBRE (g)	SOD. (mg)	POT. (mg)	IRON (mg)	CAFF. (mg)	THEOB. (mg)
¼pint/150ml water	—	—	—	—	—	—	—	—	—	—
2oz/50g unsalted butter	365	—	41	0.2	—	435	7	0.1	—	—
3oz/75g 81% wholemeal flour	245	52	1.5	9.6	5.6	3	210	1.9	—	—
2 free-range eggs	197	—	14.6	16.5	—	187	187	2.7	—	—
Chantilly piping cream										
½oz/12g gelatine	41	—	—	10	—	—	—	—	—	—
4 tbsps water	—	—	—	—	—	—	—	—	—	—
8oz/225g strained Greek yoghurt	290	8.6	18	16.4	—	152	480	—	—	—
2 drops natural vanilla essence	—	—	—	—	—	—	—	—	—	—
1 free-range egg white	15	—	—	3.8	—	80	63	0.042	—	—
Hot carob sauce										
1 × 60g bar no-added-sugar plain carob	296	25.2	19.4	6.8	0.4	117	328.8	4.8	—	—
4 tbsps skimmed milk	20	30	0.06	2	—	33	90	0.03	—	—
1 tbsp skimmed milk powder	101	15	0.37	10.4	—	157	471	0.11	—	—
Total	**1570**	**130.8**	**94.93**	**75.7**	**6.0**	**1164**	**1836.8**	**9.682**	—	—

Chocolate Profiteroles

	CALS. (g)	CARB. (g)	FAT (g)	PROT. (g)	FIBRE (g)	SOD. (mg)	POT. (mg)	IRON (mg)	CAFF. (mg)	THEOB. (mg)
4oz/100g white flour	350	80	1.2	9.8	3.4	2	140	2.4	—	—
8fl.oz/250ml water	—	—	—	—	—	—	—	—	—	—
2oz/50g butter	365	—	41	0.2	—	435	7	0.1	—	—
pinch of salt	—	—	—	—	—	777	—	0.004	—	—
1 egg yolk	67.8	—	6	3.2	—	10	24	1.22	—	—
2 eggs	197	—	14.6	16.5	—	187	187	2.7	—	—
Filling										
8fl.oz/250ml double cream	804.6	3.6	86.76	1.2	—	48.6	142.2	0.32	—	—
1oz/25g caster sugar	98.5	25	—	—	—	—	0.5	—	—	—
vanilla essence	—	—	—	—	—	—	—	—	—	—
Chocolate sauce										
4oz/100g plain chocolate	525	64.8	29.2	4.7	—	11	300	2.4	0.06	0.35
7oz/200g white sugar	689.5	175	—	—	—	—	3.5	—	—	—
4fl.oz/120ml water	—	—	—	—	—	—	—	—	—	—
pinch of salt	—	—	—	—	—	777	—	—	—	—
1 tsp vanilla essence	—	—	—	—	—	—	—	—	—	—
Total	**3097.4**	**348.4**	**178.76**	**35.6**	**3.4**	**2247.6**	**804.2**	**9.144**	**0.06**	**0.35**

	CALS. (g)	CARB. (g)	FAT (g)	PROT. (g)	FIBRE (g)	SOD. (mg)	POT. (mg)	IRON (mg)	CAFF. (mg)	THEOB. (mg)
Carob Chip Cookies										
4oz/100g soft margarine	730	0.1	81	0.1	—	800	5	0.3	—	—
4 tbsps clear honey	288	76.4	—	0.4	—	11	51	0.4	—	—
1 free-range egg	98.5	—	7.3	8.25	—	93.5	93.5	1.35	—	—
3oz/75g walnuts	393.75	3.75	165.76	7.02	3.9	0.56	517.5	1.8	—	—
1½oz/40g sunflower seeds	210	7.4	17.73	9	0.22	21	405	2.72	—	—
1 × 60g bar no-added-sugar plain carob	296	25.2	19.4	6.8	0.4	117	328.8	4.8	—	—
6oz/175g wholemeal flour	477	98.7	3	19.5	14.4	4.5	540	1.2	—	—
1 tsp baking powder	5.82	1.35	—	0.18	—	421.5	1.75	—	—	—
Total	**2499.07**	**212.9**	**294.19**	**51.25**	**18.92**	**1469.06**	**1942.55**	**12.57**		
Chocolate Chip Cookies										
4oz/100g butter	740	—	82	0.4	—	870	15	0.2	—	—
4oz/100g brown sugar	394	100	—	0.5	—	6	89	0.9	—	—
4oz/100g granulated sugar	394	100	—	—	—	—	2	—	—	—
1 egg	98.5	—	7.3	8.25	—	93.5	93.5	1.35	—	—
5oz/150g white flour	437.5	125	1.5	12.25	4.25	2.5	175	3	—	—
½ tsp salt	—	—	—	—	—	2331	—	0.012	—	—
½ tsp baking powder	2.91	0.67	—	0.09	—	210.71	0.87	—	—	—
4oz/100g walnuts	525	5	221	10.6	5.2	3	690	2.4	—	—
6oz/175g chocolate chips	793.5	89.1	45.45	12.6	—	180	630	2.4	0.0175	0.1225
Total	**3385.41**	**419.77**	**357.25**	**44.69**	**9.45**	**3696.71**	**1695.37**	**10.262**	**0.0175**	**0.1225**

	CALS. (g)	CARB. (g)	FAT (g)	PROT. (g)	FIBRE (g)	SOD. (mg)	POT. (mg)	IRON (mg)	CAFF. (mg)	THEOB. (mg)
Boston Brownies										
4oz/100g soft margarine	730	0.1	81	0.1	—	80	5	0.3	—	—
4oz/100g muscovado sugar	394	100	—	0.5	—	6	89	0.9	—	—
2 free-range eggs	197	—	14.6	16.5	—	187	187	2.7	—	—
2oz/50g wholemeal flour	159	32.9	1	6.6	4.8	1.5	180	2	—	—
1oz/25g carob powder	50.57	13.14	0.7	1.2	2	28.57	271.42	14.28	—	—
1 tsp baking powder	5.82	1.35	—	0.18	—	421.42	1.75	—	—	—
3oz/75g walnuts	393.75	3.75	38.62	7.02	3.9	2.25	517.5	1.8	—	—
9 walnut halves	131.25	1.25	55.25	2.39	1.3	0.18	172.5	0.6	—	—
1 tbsp no-added-sugar jam	30.75	8.75	—	0.08	—	3.5	19.5	0.25	—	—
Total	**2092.14**	**157.45**	**191.17**	**34.57**	**12**	**1453.42**	**1443.67**	**22.83**	—	—
Chocolate Brownies										
4oz/100g butter	740	—	82	0.4	—	870	15	0.1	—	—
4oz/100g caster sugar	394	100	—	—	—	—	2	—	—	—
2 eggs	197	—	14.6	16.5	—	187	187	2.7	—	—
2oz/50g white flour	175	40	0.6	4.9	1.7	1	70	1.2	—	—
1½oz/40g cocoa powder	133.71	4.98	9.61	6.96	—	407.1	642.85	4.5	0.13	0.74
4oz/100g walnuts	525	5	51.5	10.6	5.2	3	690	2.4	—	—
9 walnut halves	131.25	1.25	55.25	2.39	1.3	0.18	172.5	0.6	—	—
1 tsp baking powder	5.82	1.35	—	0.18	—	421.5	1.75	—	—	—
1 tbsp jam	68.00	17.50	0.25	0.15	—	3.0	22.00	0.25	—	—
Total	**2369.75**	**170.08**	**213.81**	**42.08**	**8.2**	**1892.78**	**1803.10**	**11.75**	**0.13**	**0.74**

Carob Fudge Cake

	CALS. (g)	CARB. (g)	FAT (g)	PROT. (g)	FIBRE (g)	SOD. (mg)	POT. (mg)	IRON (mg)	CAFF. (mg)	THEOB. (mg)
1oz/25g carob powder	50.57	13.14	0.7	1.2	2	28.57	271.42	14.28	—	—
¼pint/150ml water	—	—	—	—	—	—	—	—	—	—
1½ × 60g bar no-added-sugar plain carob	444	37.8	29.1	10.2	0.6	175.5	493.2	7.2	—	—
4oz/100g soft margarine	730	0.1	81	0.1	—	800	5	0.3	—	—
4oz/100g light muscovado sugar	394	100	—	0.25	—	3	44	0.45	—	—
3 free-range eggs	295.5	—	21.9	24.75	—	280.5	280.5	4.05	—	—
1 tbsp decaffeinated coffee dissolved in 1tbsp water	—	—	—	—	—	—	—	—	—	—
8oz/225g wholemeal flour	636	131.6	4	26.4	19.2	6	720	8	—	—
Fudge frosting										
2 × 60g bars plain carob	622	64.4	39.6	6.2	0.6	87.6	399.6	7.2	—	—
8oz/225g low-fat curd cheese	219	3.2	9.14	31	—	900	108	0.2	—	—
Total	**3391.07**	**350.24**	**185.44**	**100.1**	**22.4**	**2281.17**	**2321.72**	**41.68**		

Chocolate Fudge Cake

	CALS. (g)	CARB. (g)	FAT (g)	PROT. (g)	FIBRE (g)	SOD. (mg)	POT. (mg)	IRON (mg)	CAFF. (mg)	THEOB. (mg)
1oz/25g cocoa powder	89.4	3.28	6.2	5.28	—	271.4	428.57	3	0.04	0.25
¼pint/150ml water	—	—	—	—	—	—	—	—	—	—
4oz/100g butter	740	—	82.0	0.4	—	870	15	0.2	—	—
6oz/175g brown sugar	591	—	—	0.75	—	9	133	1.35	—	—
8oz/225g white flour	700	160	2.4	19.6	—	4	280	4.8	—	—
1 tsp baking powder	5.82	1.35	—	0.18	—	421.42	1.75	—	—	—
3 eggs	295.5	—	21.9	24.75	—	280.5	280.5	4.05	—	—
8fl.oz/250ml soured cream	487.6	7.36	48.76	5.52	—	96.6	276	0.7	—	—
4oz/100g milk chocolate	529	59.4	30.3	8.4	—	120	420	2.4	0.01	0.07
Fudge frosting										
2¼oz/60g plain chocolate	795	96	45	7.05	—	33	900	7.2	0.036	0.21
3fl.oz/90ml milk	19.8	3	0.06	2.04	—	31.2	90	0.03	—	—
10oz/275g caster sugar	985	250	—	—	—	5	5	—	—	—
2oz/50g butter	365	—	41	0.2	—	435	7	0.1	—	—
1 tbsp golden syrup	74	25	—	0.075	—	67	60	0.375	—	—
Total	**5677.12**	**605.39**	**1015.62**	**74.245**	**—**	**2639.12**	**2896.82**	**24.205**	**0.086**	**0.53**

	CALS. (g)	CARB. (g)	FAT (g)	PROT. (g)	FIBRE (g)	SOD. (mg)	POT. (mg)	IRON (mg)	CAFF. (mg)	THEOB. (mg)
Carob Mousse										
2 free-range eggs	197	—	14.6	16.5	—	187	187	2.7	—	—
2 tbsps clear honey	144	38.2	—	0.2	—	5.5	25.5	0.2	—	—
½pint/300ml skimmed milk	66	10	0.2	6.8	—	104	300	0.1	—	—
½oz/12g gelatine	41	—	—	10	—	—	—	—	—	—
4 tbsps boiling water	—	—	—	—	—	—	—	—	—	—
2 × 60g bars no-added-sugar plain carob	592	50.4	38.8	13.6	0.8	234	657.6	9.6	—	—
8oz/225g skimmed-milk soft cheese	166	5.4	1	33	—	900	108	0.2	—	—
Total	**1206**	**104**	**54.6**	**80.1**	**0.8**	**1482.5**	**142.81**	**12.8**	—	—
Chocolate Mousse										
4oz/100g plain chocolate	525	64.8	29.2	4.7	—	11	300	2.4	0.06	0.35
4 tbsps water	—	—	—	—	—	—	—	—	—	—
½oz/12g gelatine	41	—	—	10	—	—	—	—	—	—
3 eggs	295.5	—	21.9	24.75	—	280.5	280.5	4.05	—	—
¼pint/150ml double cream	514.05	2.3	55.43	1.725	—	31.05	90.85	0.23	—	—
Total	**1375.55**	**67.1**	**106.53**	**41.175**	—	**322.55**	**671.35**	**6.68**	**0.06**	**0.35**

	CALS. (g)	CARB. (g)	FAT (g)	PROT. (g)	FIBRE (g)	SOD. (mg)	POT. (mg)	IRON (mg)	CAFF. (mg)	THEOB. (mg)
Carob Digestives										
4oz/100g wholemeal flour	318	65.8	2	13.2	9.6	3	360	4	—	—
½ tsp baking powder	2.91	0.67	—	0.09	—	210.71	0.87	—	—	—
1oz/25g light muscovado sugar	98	25	—	0.125	—	1.5	22	0.11	—	—
2oz/50g medium oatmeal	200	31.4	4.35	6.2	3.5	16.5	185	2.05	—	—
2oz/50g soft margarine	365	—	40.05	0.05	—	400	2.5	0.1	—	—
2 tbsps skimmed milk	10	15	0.02	1	—	17	45	0.14	—	—
1 × 60g plain carob bar	311	32.2	19.8	3.1	0.3	43.8	199.8	3.6	—	—
Total	**1304.91**	**170.07**	**66.22**	**23.765**	**13.4**	**692.51**	**815.17**	**10**	—	—
Chocolate Digestives										
3oz/75g wholemeal flour	238.5	49.35	1.5	9.9	7.2	2.25	270	3	—	—
1oz/25g white flour	87.5	16.45	0.3	2.45	0.85	0.5	35	0.6	—	—
1oz/25g medium oatmeal	100	15.52	2.18	3.1	1.52	8.25	92.5	1.02	—	—
1 tsp baking powder	5.82	1.35	—	0.18	—	421.42	1.75	—	—	—
½ tsp salt	—	—	—	—	—	2331	—	0.012	—	—
1oz/25g brown sugar	98	25	—	0.125	—	1.5	22	0.225	—	—
2oz/50g butter	365	—	41	0.2	—	435	7	0.1	—	—
2 tbsps milk	21	1.5	1.2	1.1	—	16.6	50	0.01	—	—
2oz/50g plain chocolate	265	32	15	2.35	—	11	300	2.4	0.03	0.175
Total	**1180.82**	**141.17**	**61.18**	**19.405**	**9.57**	**3227.52**	**778.25**	**7.367**	**0.03**	**0.175**

Carob Eclairs

	CALS. (g)	CARB. (g)	FAT (g)	PROT. (g)	FIBRE (g)	SOD. (mg)	POT. (mg)	IRON (mg)	CAFF. (mg)	THEOB. (mg)
¼pint/150ml water	—	—	—	—	—	—	—	—	—	—
2oz/50g unsalted butter	370	—	41	0.2	—	3.5	7.5	0.08	—	—
3oz/75g 81% wholemeal flour	245	52	1.5	9.6	5.6	3	210	1.9	—	—
2 free-range eggs	197	—	14.6	16.5	—	187	187	2.7	—	—
Filling										
8oz/225g strained Greek yoghurt	290	8.6	18	16.4	—	152	480	0.2	—	—
½oz/12g gelatine	41	—	—	10	—	—	—	—	—	—
4 tbsps water	—	—	—	—	—	—	—	—	—	—
1 free-range egg white	15	—	—	3.8	—	80	63	0.042	—	—
Topping										
1 × 60g bar no-added-sugar plain carob	296	25.2	19.4	6.8	0.4	117	328.8	4.8	—	—
2 tbsps skimmed milk	10	15	0.03	1	—	17	45	0.015	—	—
Total	**1464**	**100.8**	**94.53**	**74**	**8**	**559.5**	**1228.3**	**9.82**	**—**	**—**

Chocolate Eclairs

	CALS. (g)	CARB. (g)	FAT (g)	PROT. (g)	FIBRE (g)	SOD. (mg)	POT. (mg)	IRON (mg)	CAFF. (mg)	THEOB. (mg)
4oz/100g white flour	350	80	1.2	9.8	3.4	2	140	2.4	—	—
8fl.oz/240ml water	—	—	—	—	—	—	—	—	—	—
2oz/50g butter	370	—	41	0.4	—	7	15	0.16	—	—
pinch of salt	—	—	—	—	—	777	—	0.004	—	—
1 egg yolk	67.8	—	6	3.2	—	10	24	1.22	—	—
2 eggs	197	—	14.6	16.5	—	187	187	2.7	—	—
Filling										
8fl.oz/240ml double cream	1005	4.5	108.4	3.3	—	60.75	177	0.45	—	—
1oz/25g caster sugar	98.5	25	—	—	—	—	5	—	—	—
3 drops vanilla essence	—	—	—	—	—	—	—	—	—	—
Topping										
2oz/50g plain chocolate	265	32	15	2.35	—	5.5	150	1.2	0.03	0.175
1 tsp water	—	—	—	—	—	—	—	—	—	—
½oz/12g butter	92.5	—	10	1	—	2	4	0.4	—	—
4oz/100g icing sugar	394	100	—	—	—	—	2	—	—	—
Total	**2839**	**241.5**	**196.1**	**35.65**	**3.4**	**1049.25**	**699.5**	**8.53**	**0.03**	**0.175**

Carob Ice-Cream

	CALS. (g)	CARB. (g)	FAT (g)	PROT. (g)	FIBRE (g)	SOD. (mg)	POT. (mg)	IRON (mg)	CAFF. (mg)	THEOB. (mg)
½pint/300ml skimmed milk	66	10	0.2	6.8	—	104	300	0.1	—	—
2 free-range eggs	197	—	14.6	16.5	—	187	187	2.7	—	—
1 tbsp fructose	93	25	—	—	—		—	—	—	—
1 × 60g bar plain carob	311	32.2	19.8	3.1	0.3	43.8	199.8	3.6	—	—
4oz/100g quark	75	1.4	1.5	12.1	—	450	54	0.1		
Total	**742**	**68.6**	**36.1**	**38.5**	**0.3**	**774.8**	**640.8**	**6.55**	—	—

Chocolate Ice-Cream

	CALS. (g)	CARB. (g)	FAT (g)	PROT. (g)	FIBRE (g)	SOD. (mg)	POT. (mg)	IRON (mg)	CAFF. (mg)	THEOB. (mg)
½pint/300ml milk	130	9.4	7.6	6.6	—	100	300	0.1	—	—
2 free-range eggs	197	—	14.6	15.5	—	187	187	2.7	—	—
2½oz/65g granulated sugar	246.25	62.5	—	—	—		1.25	—	—	—
3oz/75g plain chocolate	393.74	48.6	21.9	3.52	—	8.25	225	1.8	0.045	0.26
6fl.oz/180ml double cream	771	3.45	83.14	2.58	—	46.57	136.27	0.345	—	—
Total	**1737.99**	**123.95**	**127.24**	**29.2**	**—**	**341.82**	**849.52**	**4.945**	**0.045**	**0.26**

Carob Sachertorte

	CALS. (g)	CARB. (g)	FAT (g)	PROT. (g)	FIBRE (g)	SOD. (mg)	POT. (mg)	IRON (mg)	CAFF. (mg)	THEOB. (mg)
4oz/100g soft margarine	730	0.1	81	0.1	—	800	5	0.3	—	—
3oz/75g fructose	281	75	—	—	—	—	—	—	—	—
1½ × 60g bars no-added-sugar plain carob	444	37.8	94.09	10.2	0.6	175.5	493.2	7.2	—	—
3 free-range eggs	295.5	—	21.9	24.75	—	280.5	280.5	4.05	—	—
4oz/100g wholemeal flour	318	65.8	2	13.2	9.6	3	360	4	—	—
Carob ganache										
2 × 60g bars no-added-sugar plain carob	622	64.4	39.6	6.2	0.6	234	657.6	9.6	—	—
¼pint/150ml single cream	243.8	3.68	24.38	2.76	—	48.3	138	0.35	—	—
Total	**2934.3**	**246.78**	**262.97**	**57.21**	**10.8**	**1541.3**	**1934.3**	**25.5**	—	—

Chocolate Sachertorte

	CALS. (g)	CARB. (g)	FAT (g)	PROT. (g)	FIBRE (g)	SOD. (mg)	POT. (mg)	IRON (mg)	CAFF. (mg)	THEOB. (mg)
4oz/100g butter	740	—	82	0.4	—	870	15	0.2	—	—
3oz/75g icing sugar	295.5	75	—	—	—	—	1.5	—	—	—
5 eggs	492.5	—	36.5	41.25	—	467.5	467.5	1.35	—	—
3oz/75g caster sugar	295.5	75	—	—	—	—	1.5	—	—	—
4oz/100g plain chocolate	525	64.8	29.2	4.7	3.4	11	300	2.4	0.06	0.35
4oz/100g white flour	350	80	1.2	9.8	3.4	2	140	2.4	—	—
Chocolate ganache										
8oz/225g plain chocolate	1050	129.6	58.4	9.4	—	22	600	4.8	0.135	0.7875
¼ pint/150ml single cream	243.8	3.68	24.38	2.76	—	48.3	138	0.35	—	—
Total	**3992.3**	**428.08**	**231.68**	**68.31**	**3.4**	**1420.8**	**1663.5**	**11.50**	**0.195**	**1.1375**

Index

additives 12, 13
Advisory Committee, MAFF
    10
agar agar 18
algaroba 14
allergens 7, 11
Almond Clusters 60
    Log, Carob and 43
astralagus gummifer 14
Australia 17
Aztecs 8, 11

baking powder 18
Banana Cake 45
    frosting 42
    Mousse 81
    Muffins 105
Bars, Carob-coated Crunch
    104
    Raisin 105
Bavarian Carob Cake 41
Birthday Cake, Carob 108
biscuits 28, 49–58 *see*
    individual headings, also
    Cookies
Black Forest Gâteau 20–1
Blackcurrant and Carob Mint
    Chip Ice-Cream 102
Blancmange, Carob 107
blood pressure 12
Bombe, Carob 100
breast disease 10
Brioche, Carob 37
Brownies, Boston 24
    Gooey 44
butter 17

Cadbury, John 8
caffeine 7, 9, 10, 12, 17
cakes 26–7, 35–48 *see*
    individual headings
calcium 7, 10–11, 12
carob *(ceratonia siliqua)* 7,
    12–17, 96
    bars 14, 16
    caraque 21, 96
    chips 16
    composition of 12
    cream 53, 57
    curls 96
    drinking 112
    frosting 27, 36, 77, 78
    ganache 25, 108

history of 14–15
    leaves 93, 96
    oil of 14
    processing 13–14
    sauce 23, 80
    shapes 33, 96
    spread 73, 74
    use in cooking 15–16
Carob and Almond Log 43
Carob and Cinnamon
    Crumble Cake 48
Carob Chip Cake 37
Carob Ice-Cream 29, 100, 113
    Chip 80, 101
    Praline 101
Carob Slices 78
Carrot Cake 42
Chantilly Piping Cream 21,
    23, 33, 41, 76, 93
    how to make 23, 41
cheese 12, 18
cheesecake 18
    Baked Carob 94
    Orange 95
    Peach and Carob 79
chestnut filling 89
    frosting 43
    Roll 84
Chequerboards, Carob 54
children's corner 103–10 *see*
    individual headings
chocolate 7–12
    and disease 9–11
    and spots 7, 10–11
    as aphrodisiac 11–12
    composition of 8–12
    consumption of 7–8
    history of 8
cholesterol 9
choux pastry 17, 22–3, 87
Cinnamon Crumble Cake,
    Carob and 48
Coconut Castles 65
coffee 8, 9, 10, 18
    and Walnut Gâteau 36
Confectioner's Custard 67
Cookies, Carob Chip 32
    Refrigerator 50
cream 18

Cream Sandwiches, Carob 53
Crêpes, Carob 89
Croissants 73
Cyprus 13

Date Cups 61
desserts 22–3, 33, 75–96 *see*
    individual headings
DHSS 10
diabetes 9
Digestives, Carob 28
drinks 8, 9, 111–13
Dumb-bells 57

Ebionites 15
Eclairs, Carob 30–1
Egyptians 14, 15
essences 18

fats 9, 10, 11, 17
fibre, 10, 12, 17
fillings 21, 23, 31, 38, 40, 53,
    57, 88, 89, 90, 94
Flapjacks, Carob 109
flavourings, artificial 18
flour 11, 17
France/French 8
frosting 26, 27, 36, 39, 42, 43,
    47, 77, 108
    how to make 27, 42, 47, 77
fructose 17
Fry, John 8
Fudge Cake 26–7
    Fingers 104

ganache *see* carob
Gâteau, Black Forest 20–1
    Carob Mousse 90–1
    Coffee and Walnut 36
    Hazelnut 77
gelatine 18
Gelozone 18
Ginger Biscuits 55
    Sponge Fingers 51
Greece 13, 14
gum, carob/locust bean 13–14

Hazelnut Biscuits 50
    Gâteau 77
    Hearts 51
Health Education Council 10
heart disease 9
Hills, Lawrence D. 16–17

honey 17
hypoglycaemia 10

ice-cream 18, 29, 97–102 see
    individual headings
    how to make 98–9
insulin 10
Israel 9
Italy 13

jams 18
Japs 64
Junket, Carob 106

Kalibu 15

Lemon Sponge 38
lecithin 14
lignin 12
lipase 14

Macaroons, Carob 62
Madeleines, Carob 69
margarines 17
Marzipan Slices 70–1
Mediterranean 13, 17
Mexico 8, 11
migraines 7, 11, 12
mint-carob 92, 101, 102, 113
Mint and Carob Chip Moulds
    62
    Coeur à la Creme 92
    Shake 113
    Thins 56
Mocha Ice-Cream 102
    Pots 82
    Ring 39
monoamine oxidases 12
Mousse 18
    Carob 33
    Carob Banana 81
    Carob Gâteau 90–1
    Tia 76
Muffins, banana 105
Munchies, muesli 107

Norway 9

nutritional content 17, 20, 22,
    24, 25, 27–30 passim, 32,
    33

Oaties, Carob 52
Orange and Carob Marble
    Loaf, 44
    Cheesecake 95
osteomalacia 11
osteoporosis 11
ovens, microwave 16, 99
oxalic acid 7, 11, 12

Pain au Carob 74
Palestine 13
Passion Cake 47
Patisserie 63–74 see
    individual headings
Peach and Carob Cheesecake
    79
    Roulade 88
Pear Frangipane 68
Pears, Carob 86
pectin 12
Petits Fours 59–62 see
    individual headings
    Piped 61
Petits Pots au Carob 93
phenylethylamine 7, 11–12
phosphorus 12
Pineapple Pie 85
Poire Belle Helène 80
Popcorn, Carob 106
potassium 12
pregnancy 10
Profiteroles, Carob 22–3

Raisin Bars 105
Raspberry 'Choc' Ice 99
Rations for Livestock 17
rickets 11
Ring, Mocha 39
    Strawberry Choux 87
Roulade, Carob Peach 88
Roux, Michel 90

Sachertorte, Carob 25
salt 12, 17, 18

Sarah's Carob Cake 40
shakes 112–13
    Carob Bar 112
    Carob Milk 112
    Minty 113
Shortbread, Carob 53
sieving 16, 18
sodium 12
soufflés 18
    Cold Carob 83
    Hot Carob 82
Spain/Spaniards 8, 13
spots 7, 10–11
Squares, Carob 52
stimulants 9–10
Strawberry Choux Ring 87
sugar 7, 8, 10–12 passim, 14,
    16, 17
    blood 9–10
    raw cane 14, 16–18 passim
Swiss Buns 64
    Roll 46

Tart, Carob Fruit 66–7
tea 8, 9, 10
tempering 16
theobromine 7, 9, 10, 12, 17
tooth decay 11
Toscaner, Carob 72
Truffles, De Luxe 60
tyramine 7, 11–12

United States 10, 13
    National Institute for
    Dental Research 11

Viennese Fingers 65
vitamins 9, 12, 73, 74

Walnut and Coffee Gâteau 36
    Clusters 60
wine 8, 12

xanthine 9

yoghurt 18

zinc 7, 11

Index

128